CQ Jamboree

60 years of connecting Scouts in the
Jamboree-on-the-Air
1957-2017

"CQ Jamboree" is based on the memorandum "The first Thirty Years, a personal account of the Jamboree-On-The-Air 1958-1987", written by Len Jarrett in December 1987. Les Mitchell wrote the introduction to it. Richard Middelkoop, who took over the pen from Len as editor of the annual World JOTA Report provided further information and compiled some participation statistics for the first publication in 1993 in a booklet entitled "The JOTA Story".

On the occasion of the 50th JOTA, Richard Middelkoop wrote a new booklet with the update for the subsequent years up to 2007 and published the first edition of "CQ Jamboree" (ISBN 978-90-812601-1-4) early 2008.

The current edition adds another 10 years in the log, up to the 60th JOTA. Richard has further researched material that surfaced during the latest move of the World Scout Bureau from Geneva to Kuala Lumpur and from other sources. He discovered some new twists to the JOTA story. This booklet shows historic photographs and information that have not been published before. It completes the story of "Connecting Scouts". Up to now……

CQ Jamboree

60 years of connecting Scouts in the
Jamboree-on-the-Air
1957-2017

by

RICHARD MIDDELKOOP

with introductions by LES MITCHELL and LEN JARRETT

R & M Productions
May 2018

CIP data:
Author: Middelkoop, Richard.
Title: CQ Jamboree.
Subtitle: 60 years of Connecting Scouts in the Jamboree On The Air.
Description: print-on-demand paperback edition, 2018.
Identifiers: ISBN 978-90-812601-0-7
Subjects: Youth Movement | Amateur Radio | Technical education | inter-cultural exchange | International youth community | largest world-wide youth gathering | voice of young people.

Copyright © 2018 by the author.

All rights reserved. No part of this book may be reproduced by any mechanical, photographic or electronic process in the form of photographic or scanned recording, nor may it be stored in a retrieval system, transmitted or otherwise be copied for public or private use without the prior written permission of the copyright holder.

1st edition 2008

2nd updated and revised edition 2018

ISBN 978-90-812601-0-7

NUR 680

Cover design: Marjolein Middelkoop

Published by *R&M Productions*

About the authors:

"The early days"

Les Mitchell, G3BHK, was a Scoutmaster at the time of the Jubilee Jamboree in Sutton Coldfield in 1957. It was at this event that he initiated the idea of an annual get-together for Scout radio amateurs. He organized the first meeting on the air in 1958. The event soon grew into global proportions and Les turned the organization over to the Boy Scouts World Bureau, at the time based in London. He remained the national JOTA Organizer for the UK Scout Association until 1988. Les Mitchell received the Bronze Wolf Award in 1978. Since 6 October 2014 he is a silent key.

"The first thirty years"

Len F. Jarrett, VE3MYF, was the Director of Administration of the World Scout Bureau for nearly 30 years, serving in England, Canada and Switzerland as the Bureau changed location. He resigned as a full-time employee in 1981 and was subsequently employed, on a part-time basis, as a consultant, working from his home in Canada and making periodic trips back to Geneva for another three years. After that, he worked on JOTA in a volunteer capacity. Len Jarrett received the Bronze Wolf Award in 1973.

He has been involved in the Jamboree-On-The-Air from its inception and has acted as World JOTA Organizer from the 2nd JOTA in 1959 until the 31st JOTA in 1988. Len's key is silent since 15 December 2017.

"Another thirty years"

Richard Middelkoop, PA3BAR, has been involved with the JOTA since 1976. First on a group- and regional level, from 1982 onwards in the national JOTA organization team in The Netherlands. In 1988 he was appointed as a volunteer consultant to the World Scout Bureau in Geneva. In his capacity as World JOTA Organizer, he wrote the annual World JOTA Report and was involved in the amateur-radio and communication activities at World Scout Jamborees. Richard Middelkoop received the Bronze Wolf Award in 1996. In 2013 he was appointed World JOTA-JOTI Organizer of the combined event and is the team leader of the new World JOTA-JOTI Team up to the present day.

THE 40th JOTA calls for cutting a cake to mark the milestone in Reading, United Kingdom, in the same Scout group building where the Jamboree on the Air started 40 years ago. From left to right are Len Jarrett (Canada), the JOTA organizer for many years, Les Mitchel (UK), the founder of JOTA, and Richard Middelkoop (Netherlands), the present JOTA organizer. All three are holders of the Bronze Wolf Award.

Contents

About the authors: V

Acknowledgements IX

Jamboree On The Air XI

Introduction by Les Mitchell 1
    The Early Days - 1908-1958 1

THE FIRST THIRTY YEARS by Len Jarrett 9
    The 1st JOTA 1958 10
    The 2nd JOTA 1959 13
    The 3rd JOTA 1960 15
    A Permanent Bureau station 16
    VE3WSB makes its debut 17
    The 4th JOTA 1961 17
    The 5th JOTA 1962 18
    The 6th JOTA 1963 18
    The 7th JOTA 1964 19
    The 8th JOTA 1965 20
    The 9th JOTA 1966 21
    The 10th JOTA 1967 22
    The 11th JOTA 1968 23
    The 12th JOTA 1969 23
    HB9S appears 24
    The 13th JOTA 1970 25
    The 14th JOTA 1971 25
    The 15th JOTA 1972 26
    The 16th JOTA 1973 27
    The 17th JOTA 1974 27
    The 18th JOTA 1975 28
    The 19th JOTA 1976 28
    The 20th JOTA 1977 29
    The 21st JOTA 1978 29
    The 22nd JOTA 1979 30
    The 23rd JOTA 1980 30
    The 24th JOTA 1981 31
    The 25th JOTA 1982 32
    The 26th JOTA 1983 32
    The 27th JOTA 1984 33
    The 28th JOTA 1985 34
    The 29th JOTA 1986 34
    The 30th JOTA 1987 35

ANOTHER THIRTY YEARS by Richard Middelkoop 36
    The 31st JOTA, 1988 36

- The 32nd JOTA 1989 37
- The 33rd JOTA 1990 37
- The 34th JOTA 1991 38
- The 35th JOTA 1992 39
- The 36th JOTA 1993 40
- The 37th JOTA 1994 41
- The 38th JOTA 1995 42
- The 39th JOTA 1996 42
- The new era of electronic communication 44
- The 40th JOTA 1997 44
- The 41st JOTA 1998 46
- The 42nd JOTA 1999 46
- The 43rd JOTA 2000 47
- The 44th JOTA 2001 48
- The 45th JOTA 2002 49
- The 46th JOTA 2003 50
- Amateur Radio and beyond 51
- The 47th JOTA 2004 52
- The 48th JOTA 2005 52
- Changes at the Bureau 53
- The 49th JOTA 2006 53
- The 50th JOTA 2007 55
- The 51st JOTA 2008 56
- The 52nd JOTA 2009 57
- The 53rd JOTA 2010 58
- The 54th JOTA 2011 59
- The 55th JOTA 2012 60
- The 56th JOTA 2013 62
- Merge and Move 63
- 9M4WSB appears 64
- The 57th JOTA 2014 64
- The 58th JOTA 2015 65
- A few more changes 66
- The 59th JOTA 2016 67
- The 60th JOTA 2017 68

The World Scout Bureau station 70

JOTA Reports and stories 75

Amateur Radio at World Scout Jamborees 77

A quick look into the future 94

Amateur Radio and Scouting Language 97

Acknowledgements

Special thanks for searching historic archives and the courtesy to use their materials to:

> Maurice le Pesant, F8WBE, NJC France (1947 World Scout Jamboree)
>
> Georg Haberfellner, OE3GHO, NJC Austria, and the Austrian Scout Archive and Museum (1951 World Scout Jamboree)
>
> Andrew Dunn, VE3XAD, NJC Canada, and the Scouts Canada National Museum (1955 World Scout Jamboree)
>
> Nas Ona, DU1ON, (QSL material 1959 World Scout Jamboree)
>
> Michalis Michalos, Konstantinos Dassios, and Soma Hellinon Proskopon Scout Museum Service; Golden Leaves of Marathon, ed. Scouts of Greece, 1964 (1963 World Scout Jamboree)
>
> Jim Wilson, K5ND, NJC USA, and the Boy Scouts of America archives (1967 World Scout Jamboree)
>
> Tatsuo Mochiki, JH1FEL and the Scout Association of Japan archives (1971 World Scout Jamboree)

Special thanks also to:
> the relatives of the late Les Mitchell and Len Jarrett for the continued use of their materials published in the previous editions.

Further materials courtesy of:
> World Scout Bureau archives.
>
> Personal archive material of the author.

The support of my XYL Miriam with text reviews and suggestions and her involvement in Radio-Scouting activities, mostly behind the scenes, over many years, has been instrumental in producing this historic overview of the world's largest international youth gathering.

x

Jamboree On The Air

When Scouts want to meet young people from another country they usually think of attending a World Scout Jamboree or another international gathering. But few people realise that each year in the third full weekend of October over one-and-a-half-million Scouts "get together" for the annual Jamboree-On-The-Air (JOTA). Using the modern communication technology that amateur radio stations offer, Scouts have the exciting opportunity to make friends in other countries without even leaving home. They exchange greetings with other Scouts, learn about each other's country and culture, swap programme ideas and discuss actual themes in society. JOTA is the largest annual youth gathering on earth, where the voices of young people of all nations are heard.

Since 1958 when the first Jamboree-On-The-Air was held, millions of Scouts, and in many countries also Guides, have "met" each other through this event. Not only is it fun to talk to Scouts from other parts of the world but it provides the youngsters with a chance to find out about other countries and about Scouting elsewhere. Many contacts made during the JOTA have resulted in pen pals and links between Scout troops that have lasted for many years.

With no restrictions on age or the numbers which can participate, and at little or no expense, the Jamboree-On-The-Air provides an opportunity for Scouts to contact each other by amateur radio. The radio stations are operated by licensed radio amateurs, people who studied radio techniques and passed an examination with their country's telecommunication authorities. Many Scouts and Scout leaders hold licenses themselves and operate their own stations. But the majority participates in the JOTA through stations operated by local radio amateurs. Almost all countries allow the Scouts to speak over the radio directly, even though they are not licensed themselves.

The Jamboree-On-The-Air offers Scouts the opportunity to communicate with others on a world-wide scale. Can you imagine a better way to get the feeling of belonging to a really big movement and to contribute to mutual understanding and respect?

Author's note:

Whilst every effort has been made, with the help of modern technology, to present the best quality in graphics of the historic materials, I have to accept that some photos and participation cards are clearly effected by time. In view of their historic relevance, I have chosen to present them anyway, so the history may be complete.

Richard Middelkoop

Introduction by Les Mitchell

The Early Days - 1908-1958

Even today one still meets those who consider the introduction of radio and electronic activities into our Movement as somehow alien and not in keeping with the original theme of Scouting. It will no doubt surprise them to learn that B.P. was most enthusiastic and encouraged Scouts to take up radio right from the beginning.

The 1913 edition of the British magazine "Wireless World" contained details of a scheme where the Marconi Company offered to give free instruction in wireless telegraphy to members of youth movements. B.P.'s comments concerning this were recorded as follows - "Wireless has become a favourite hobby with boys of the right kind, and it is a valuable hobby for them, because it has a big future before it... I hope that Boy Scouts, at any rate, will make full use of this opportunity thus given them, and will by their good work and progress in efficiency repay such kind interest".

Even before the above information appeared we find that the 1st Arundel Troop in Sussex had their own amateur station "on the air" in 1911. The transmitter was of the spark variety and the whole station was carefully constructed from what one would consider today to be absolute junk. They installed a 300 foot long aerial using the local brewery chimney as a mast and had the call sign "XBS". Using 200 meters they had a receiving range of 800 miles and a sending range of 5 miles.

At one of their summer camps they charged members of the public three pence each to listen to the signals from the very few commercial stations in operation - all using the Morse code.

In 1913 the "Wireless World" also published further information concerning Scout radio activities. Scouts of the 1st Kingston Troop, Surrey, had constructed a receiver which "works exceedingly well and messages have been received over long distances".

In this same year an article appeared detailing the activities of the Stockwell Scouts: *"We have a wireless telegraphy apparatus in our troop of Boy Scouts and there is no doubt concerning its popularity. This is not a toy set but a real complete double station with a range of 10 miles (for we have tested it at that), and probably even further under favourable conditions, and double the distance at night".*

Every Scout has to know 'Morse' well enough before he is admitted into the 'wireless patrol', and no one can get through with just a knowledge of the alphabet, for he has to transmit and receive, and that soon shows up weak points in his harness. I am so old now I can remember listening to 2LO on my parents crystal set back in the late 1920's.

CQ Jamboree

There is nothing like a wireless set

But for real good sport in Scouting there is nothing like a 'wireless' set. We always take ours with us. It takes less than 10 minutes to erect. The mast is of aluminium poles which fit together, and the aerial spreads out like an umbrella.
"Two stations are packed up in the trek cart ready for transport. We get along all right on the road, but some railway companies try to charge us the same rate as for a Maxim gun or a motor car for our trek cart. We are going to take it to pieces next time and sew it up in canvas! Each station can be easily carried by four to six Scouts, but we prefer to let the trek cart patrol take it for us, for it gives them exercise. The wireless patrol work it by themselves, and someday they are going to report a final cup tie or 'Varsity' boat race direct to some newspaper office to show what they can do."

This was probably one of the first semi-mobile portable amateur radio stations in the world and, of course, all of the above incidents took place prior to the establishment of broadcasting.

At this point in our story World War I took place, bringing a halt to amateur radio operations in many countries. Between this and World War II there appears to have been little radio activity within the Movement despite B.P.'s continued enthusiasm, for in 1922 he wrote - "What is going to be the most popular stunt among boys? Watch radio work and its development."

There is no doubt that it was a combination of circumstances which led to this apparent lack of Scout interest. During WWI spark transmission had given way to the use of valves (tubes to North Americans) and more sophisticated circuitry. With the advent of broadcasting in the early 1920's the amateurs had been allocated higher frequencies. Radio had reached the stage where components were expensive especially for high frequencies, and with the advancement of technology it was becoming more and more difficult to build transmitters and receivers in comparison with the days of spark.

Authorities introduce restrictions

With improved equipment, signals were reaching further and further, and it became necessary for the authorities to introduce numerous restrictions on all those involved in radio transmission. In addition the radio telegraph companies did not want listeners intercepting their messages, and many authorities made it illegal to divulge information received outside the broadcast and amateur bands.

The construction and use of transmitters by Boy Scouts themselves had become virtually impossible and really the only avenue open to them was to construct receivers. Many did just this, but, apart from listening to broadcast and amateur transmissions, they could be used for no other purpose. The signalling aspect of the spark days had gone and Scouts could no longer practise their Morse actually "on the air". The fun had gone to be replaced by a more passive listening activity.
So we come to my small part in the story. As a pre-World War II Sea Scout I joined the Royal Navy in 1942 and was trained in radio. During my naval service I

spent a year in the U.S.A. and another in Australia, becoming a Scout Leader in both countries. So, whilst sampling the international aspects of Scouting, I received training in radio which was to lead to my becoming a radio amateur after the War. When I did become a peace-time radio amateur, what struck me was the similarity between both these organizations in the friendly way they transcend class, creed, colour, religion and political boundaries.

Within a few years I was training Scouts in amateur radio and started to hold radio camps for the enthusiasts within my local district. In those days the license conditions were far more liberal and any person could operate a station under qualified supervision - we were almost back to the type of situation enjoyed by those early Scout operators. Every Scout could have a turn at operating and have an exciting and interesting experience.

Unfortunately, this privilege was withdrawn about 1956, and from then only the license holder could operate and speak over his equipment. (N.B. In the U.K. recent alterations to license conditions do allow non-licensed persons to speak over amateur transmitters from exhibition stations having call signs in the GB series. At present they may speak only to a limited number of countries, but it is hoped that this relaxation will gradually be extended.)

In 1957, a World Scout Jamboree was held at Sutton Park in central England, with 35,000 Scouts from 62 countries attending. Local radio amateurs installed and operated a large station under the call sign GB3SP.

Scouts and leaders were allowed to visit, as long as they stayed behind the little fence with the flower pots and kept the noise down.

More than 60 operators manned this station for the 12 days it was operational making contact with 1,712 stations in 71 countries. Despite the fact that unlicensed persons were not allowed to speak, the authorities did allow short hourly news broadcasts of which 120 were made.

While these were excellent results, it is interesting to compare them with GB3BSI which was in operation a decade later in 1967. This station was located on the site of the first ever Scout Camp of 1907 on Brownsea Island, Poole, Dorset and was completely organized and operated by nine Scouts, six of whom were licensed amateurs. This station made 935 contacts in 64 countries in 8 days of operation. It should be pointed out that, in between these two events, SSB (single sideband) equipment became generally used on amateur frequencies in place of the less efficient AM (amplitude modulation) equipment. While GB3SP was the second amateur station to operate from a World Scout Jamboree, it should be noted that the Wireless Institute of Australia operated a station for 24 hours a day at the Pan-Pacific Jamboree held at Wonga Park, Victoria, Australia in December, 1955 – 1 January, 1956.

CQ Jamboree

An effort to bring together overseas Scouts

I was very surprised by the number of overseas Scout radio amateurs attending the Jamboree and decided that some effort should be made to bring them all together. A notice in the Jamboree Newspaper resulted in daily coffee meetings during which we got to know each other and have a good rag chew. The meetings were actually held in a snack bar outside the gate, as meeting in the GB3GP radio station would produce too much "background noise" for the operators.

Towards the end of the Jamboree we were all a little sad at our impending departure, and someone casually remarked that we might try to contact each other on the air. This then developed into the idea of trying to make contact on one specific day in order to concentrate our efforts, and I was asked to make the necessary arrangements.

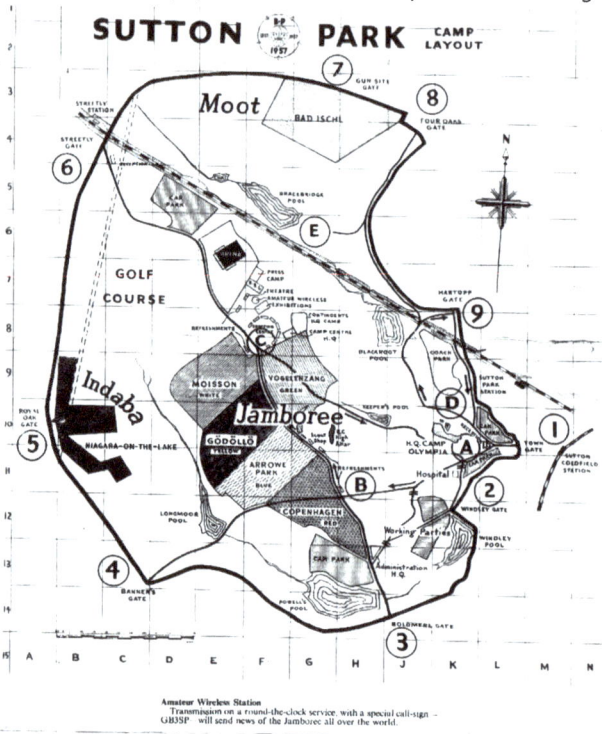

The Sutton Park Jamboree map; Radio station GB3SP is in F7 as "amateur wireless"; the coffee meetings were just outside Boldmere Gate at number 3.

When I subsequently gave this idea more detailed consideration there seemed to be a number of pitfalls. There were a few of us, and we were spread around the world. Even if everyone involved did come on on the chosen day, poor conditions could easily result in few, if any, contacts. I felt that if the first attempt ended in failure interest would quickly die, and no one would be interested in another attempt a year later.

Then the idea hit me - why not run the event for a whole weekend and ask all radio amateurs throughout the world with an interest in the Scout Movement to put

Richard Middelkoop

their stations on the air and, at the same time, invite their local Scouts to join them. Some countries still did allow non-licensed speech and, in these cases, visiting Scouts would be able to really take part themselves - thus adding much to the general interest. Even if the original "coffee meeting" Scout amateurs did fail to contact each other, it would not matter for there would be plenty of other Scout stations to talk to. I put this idea to a number of members of the original meetings, and they agreed that I should go ahead on this revised basis. So JOTA was born. (This was my own choice of title for I felt it described exactly what the event was - a Jamboree-on-the-Air.)

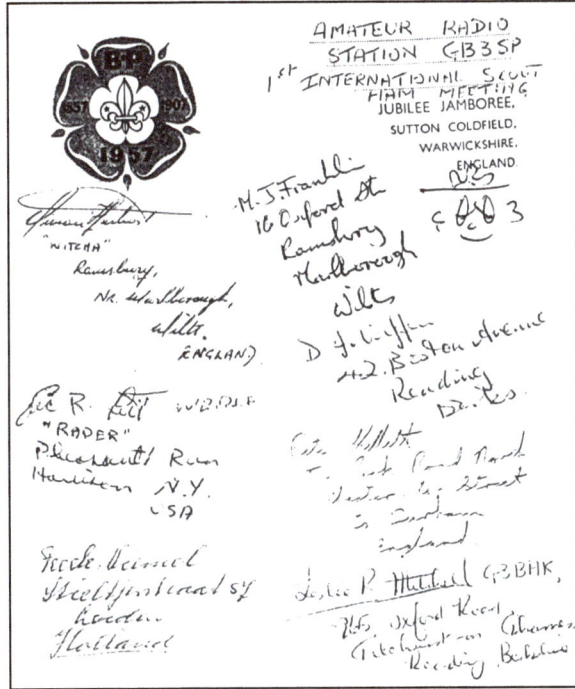

The guest book of the first ever Radio-Scouting meeting, 10 August 1957, 9th World Jamboree, Sutton Coldfield, United Kingdom.

Before launching the idea on an international basis, I felt that it would be wise to ensure that Scouts who had not been subjected to amateur radio previously would be interested in such an event. So, during October 1957, 1 organized a weekend station with my local Scout group in Reading, Berkshire. The Scouts assisted me in the installation of a station in a tent and the erection of a simple, single wire aerial. Using only a 40 watt transmitter (AM) we made contacts all over the world, and it was obvious that the interest was such that a worldwide Radio Jamboree could be envisaged. After receiving the blessing of our radio licensing authority and our National Scout H.Q., I drew up rules for the event keeping them as simple as possible. In fact, they were so simple that they have remained unchanged ever since.

The first JOTA took place 10 and 11 May 1958 and was successful despite the absence of extensive overseas support due mainly to lack of advance publicity. However, so many requests for information were received during the weekend "over the air" that it was obvious the event was its own best advertisement.

As a part-timer it did not take me long to realize that I would not be able to cope with the correspondence likely to arise in the future on a worldwide basis, and that I would have to find some permanent Scout body to take over the world organization of the event. Our U.K. International Department suggested that as it was a world event, the World Scout Bureau, then in Ottawa, Canada, might be interested. Luckily they were, for as Len was to comment later - we had a tiger by the tail! It is now past history that the event has gradually expanded to become

CQ Jamboree

the largest international event on the Scout calendar, and much credit must go to the staff of the World Scout Bureau (and especially Len) for their continued and excellent support over so many years.

While I certainly did originate JOTA, I feel I have been showered with too much credit, for I just gave the boulder a push and it gathered its own momentum as it rolled down the hillside! We must not forget, too, the thousands of individual radio amateurs who have each contributed time and effort to make JOTA enjoyable for so many years.

Now, I have brought the story up to the point where JOTA becomes a World Scout Bureau responsibility, and you must look at the rest of the history through Len Jarrett's eyes. Some call me "Father" of this event, but since the first JOTA, I have only looked after the "U.K. Kids". Len looked after the world's "JOTA children". So, it is over to you "Global Dad"... Over!

"World Scouting" - March, 1958:

COMING EVENTS

JAMBOREE-ON-THE-AIR

A Boy Scout "Jamboree-On-The-Air" will be held on May 10th-11th when all radio amateurs throughout the world who have an interest in the Scout Movement are invited to make contact with each other, as announced by the International Scout Club, London.

Stations may operate at any time from midnight on Friday, May 9th until midnight on Sunday 11th (local time) on any amateur wave-band and with any equipment which is consistent with licence regulations.

Apart from individual participation it is hoped that radio stations will be set up in group and District Headquarters and on camp-sites with the co-operation of local amateur radio societies and clubs who are being asked to assist if at all possible. All amateurs participating must strictly observe their licence regulations.

Scouts wishing to know the address of their nearest amateur radio Society or club should get in touch with their National Radio Amateur Society.

This is not a contest and there will be no prizes for the operator making the most contacts. The event is being expressly organised to further the bonds of international friendship and brotherhood which unite the Scout Movement. A special station with its own call-sign is planned to be in operation from Gilwell Park.

Enquiries regarding this event should be addressed to the Hon. Organiser, The Boy Scout Jamboree-on-the-Air, 965 Oxford Road, Tilehurst-on-Thames, Reading, Berks, England.

The Boy Scouts International Bureau will also be on the air. A friend of the Scout Movement in Ottawa has generously placed at our disposal his fine amateur station. Technical data will be supplied at a later date to all International Commissioners for distribution in their respective countries.

Richard Middelkoop

SCOUTS OVER THE AIR

Reading Leader Of Jamboree

WHEN, nearly 40 years ago, I belonged to the Scout movement, I had the tremendous adventure of hearing over a crystal set—straining my ears in the headphones—the faintest whisper of a brass band in play; it was the very first time " the wireless " had revealed its secrets to me.

On Saturday, sitting in a dingy belltent windshaken on Kentwood Hill, Tilehurst, over short-wave radio I heard Scouts in parts of Britain as far removed as Yorkshire and Dorset greeting each other, chatting and laughing with, at times, better reception than might have been experienced over similar distances with the telephone. And I thrilled to know that this was going on that day, during the night, and until noon next day not only all over this country but in many other parts of the world.

At last year's Jamboree at Sutton Coldfield, Scout instructor Mr. Leslie Mitchell, of 965, Oxford Road, Reading (attached to the 79th Reading Scout group), was chatting with fellow " hams " (short-wave radio enthusiasts) over coffee when he happened to mention what a good idea it would be to have an annual " field day," as it were, of Scout " hams." The idea was snapped up. Mr. Mitchell became honorary organiser for the first Boy Scout international Jamboree-on-the-air.

During the war, Mr. Mitchell was a petty officer in the Navy, and a radio electrician. When demobilised, he developed his war-time knowledge (and cheaply acquired ex-War Department equipment) an enthusiasm for short-wave radio. Since then his code number, G3BHK/A, and his "handie," Les, have become widely known, and he has contacted stations as remote as Guam, in the Pacific Ocean, and Okinawa.

Beneath 275ft. of wire hitched at its highest to a flagpole alongside the Group's headquarters on Saturday, Mr. Mitchell operated his 120-watt transmitter, combing the ether for Scouts and friendship. Apart from his receiver, which was ex-War Department, the whole of his £100-worth of equipment arranged inside the tent was handmade; he had, in fact, only finished building his transmitter at 9.30 that morning.

Television cramped his style as far as foreign stations were concerned, and, in any case, atmospheric conditions were far from favourable (and continued so throughout the Jamboree). But, with eager Scouts listening, he quickly made contact with Woolhampton (Douai Abbey) and Peppard Common (schoolmaster Mr A. Hutchence), and cheers and counter-cheers of salute went over the air.

All through the night the cheery chatter over microphone and loudspeaker went on. But, try as he might, he just could not " work " the central station of Gilwell Park, home of Scouting.

Moreover, foreigners were equally elusive. But, with the co-operation of Mr. John Pinchbeck, operating a non-Scout set at 20, Church End Lane, Tilehurst, Mr. Mitchell and his companions were able to exchange greetings with Auckland (New Zealand) and Tokyo, the former lasting some 45 minutes.

" I worked about 25 to 30 British stations—Scout stations," Mr. Mitchell told me " But conditions were frustrating. I hope a similar Jamboree will take place next year, and that we shall find then conditions much more favourable. This kind of thing not only furthers the spirit of unity within Scouting, but contributes much to world understanding and friendship."
—L.N.

SCOUTS BUILD RADIO STATION

" Ham " Chats With Leningrad

FROM the hillside field headquarters of the 79th Reading (Norcot and Kentwood) Scout Group, an amateur radio station operated for 24 hours at the weekend. And during that time 63 stations in 30 different countries were contacted, including Leningrad. The " best " contacts were with Japan and Okinawa.

It was a Scout-organized operation, Mr. Leslie Mitchell (G3BHK —in radio " ham " language), who has been in Scouting since 1936, being the operator, aided by schoolmaster Mr. Arthur Hutchence (G3IKA), of Peppard.

The idea grew out of the Jamboree, where there was a radio station which Mr. Mitchell, with 1st Ramsbury Senior Scouts, helped to run. It was suggested that Scouts under instruction could erect a radio station themselves and see how it operated.

The field of the 79th was ideal and, with the Ramsbury Troop, the seniors set to on Saturday. They rigged the aerial and other equipment in one-and-a-half hours, and then worked in four watches throughout the 24 hours in the operating tent They made entries in the station log book, kept a card index of stations and countries worked, made out the confirmation of contact cards—and provided a constant supply of tea for the operators !

When the equipment was switched on it was found that a world-wide radio contest was in operation, and so they joined in. The results far exceeded expectations, and the countries contacted included Chile, Canary Islands, Sicily, Bahrein Islands, Brazil, USA, Canada, USSR, Kenya, Malta, Cyprus, Sierra Leone and Libya.

The amateur in Leningrad said he hoped that the Scouts were enjoying themselves and that the camp was a success.

Newspaper clippings from the Reading Chronicle, telling the story of the first JOTA in Reading, UK; from the personal archives of Les Mitchell.

CQ Jamboree

"Popular Wireless Weekly, March 24th 1923. p151."

WIRELESS AND THE BOY SCOUTS ASSOCIATION.

By LIEUT.-GENERAL SIR ROBERT BADEN-POWELL, K.C.V.O., K.C.B., C.B., C.V.O., LL.D., F.R.G.S.

Every Thursday the London station broadcasts a talk to Scouts, and the following article, specially written by the Chief Scout for POPULAR WIRELESS, will appeal to all Scout readers.

THE recent development of wireless broadcasting in this country has added yet another means of rapid thought-communication to those which we already possess. Within a very brief period science has bequeathed to us the land-line telegraph and telephone and the wireless telegraph. To-day we are witnessing the arrival of the latest gift of science—the wireless telephone.

Hitherto, the only avenue of approach to the millions who make up society has been through the Press. Never before in the history of journalism has such an organisation existed for the dissemination of news as the modern daily Press. Yet even that has its limitations. The best daily paper in existence can only convey its news at the speed of the newsboy who races down the street with it in the city in which it is produced, or of the train or aeroplane which carries it for distribution in country districts.

The wireless telegraph has, of course, for many years played a very important part in the commercial and industrial development of all civilised communities. Its value as a means of saving life at sea has, moreover, been demonstrated over and over again since the beginning of the present century.

The scope of its utility, however, though wide, has always been restricted by the fact that it can only be used as a means of communication between specially trained operators. This, of course, puts it outside the reach—or, at any rate, the interest—of the millions.

Its Uses in Organisation

The ordinary land-line telephone is free from these two drawbacks. It lacks both the unintelligibility of the telegraph and the comparative slowness of the newspaper. It enables a straightforward message, which needs no deciphering, to be transmitted almost instantaneously over hundreds of miles. But once more there is an important limitation—the ordinary telephone cannot reach the ears of millions of people simultaneously.

In making it possible for this wonderful feat to be performed, the wireless telephone promises to exercise a more far-reaching influence over society than has been achieved by any other invention of modern times. Properly used and controlled by the individual and the State alike, it should prove a potent factor in welding the social, economic, and political interests that exist, not only among the individuals of this nation, but among the various nations that constitute this Empire.

Wireless telephony broadcasting, apart from its interest and value as a means of distributing news, music, weather reports, etc., is particularly suitable as an instrument of inter-communication, and control

in the service of such a widespread organisation as the Boy Scouts Association.

In every sphere of activity efficient organisation calls for the swiftest available means of transmitting intelligence from those in command to the members of the various sections and sub-sections under their control.

In the past even the quickest method of effecting this has always necessitated some method of "relaying" the information on from one department to another. When the different groups comprising the organisation are situated in all parts of the country, as in the case of the Boy Scouts Association, this relaying system leaves much to be desired at times, particularly in moments of sudden emergency. Wireless telephony provides a means of direct communications between all branches of the Association, and it is hoped, as opportunity offers in the future, to take fullest advantage of the facilities it affords.

Qualifying for Badges

At present, in order to qualify for a *Telegraphist* badge a Scout must understand the elementary principles of a wireless telegraph installation. Many Scouts and Scoutmasters, of course, possess a very sound knowledge of wireless principles, and, moreover, are the owners of excellent portable outfits and amateur equipments. It is hoped, however, to inaugurate a much broader scheme for wireless instruction among Scouts in the near future. Now that so many new wireless societies are coming into being throughout the country, it may be possible to arrange for local Scouts to benefit by attending their lectures and demonstrations, etc.

An *Electrician* badge, involves a knowledge of how to make a simple electro-magnet, the action of simple cells, and the working of electric bells and telephones.

An applicant for a *Pilot* badge must, among other things, be able to fix positions by means of cross bearings, an operation which is, of course, constantly involved in wireless position-finding. This, incidentally, is a branch of wireless which should prove of special interest to Scouts. Equipped with a directional aerial and a suitable chart, a Scout should be able to guide himself over any area of the country by day or by night. Not only can he set his course from observation of the direction of received signals, but he can also check his position periodically by taking cross bearings on any number of the transmitting stations which are constantly in action.

Note from Les Mitchell:

B.P. was obviously involved in broadcasting talks about the Movement as early as 1925. The London station referred to above was G2LO which commenced broadcasting from Marconi House in the Strand on the 11th May 1922.

The text of this talk printed above was at the time when Wireless telephony was just gaining popularity. This talks contains B.P.'s thoughts that it would be wonderful if Scouts could make use of this wonderful new facilty. He also mentions that wireless could be used for position finding, another useful facility to help Scouts.

So here is B.P. talking about new inventions, showing that he had thoughts about JOTA-type operations and radio orienteering, a quarter of a century before they actually became Scouting activities.

THE FIRST THIRTY YEARS by Len Jarrett

Scout interest in radio did not suddenly commence with the first Jamboree-on-the-Air in 1958, and is really as old as the Movement itself. As this involves B.P.'s own personal thoughts and much of the history revolves around activities in the United Kingdom, I have asked Les Mitchell to summarize his knowledge of the pre-1958 period and to set the scene leading up to my own introduction to the Jamboree-on-the-Air in 1958.

When Noel Lynch, upon his retirement as Australian National JOTA Organizer in 1984, sent me a copy of his Australian JOTA History, saying that he had written it so that there would be a record of the early days of JOTA in Australia, it occurred to me that I should follow suit. The World Bureau had moved from Canada to Switzerland in 1968 and records of the early years had been destroyed. I had resigned as a full-time employee in 1981, leaving nobody still on the staff who had been there when JOTA started in 1958. In the meantime, JOTA had grown into an annual event involving over a quarter of a million Scouts and Guides and over 6,000 amateur radio stations - making it both the largest World Scouting and the largest amateur radio event. So perhaps I should tell the JOTA story just for the archives of World Scouting.

The problem is, however, that there isn't just one JOTA story, rather there are 250,000 each year - for every boy or girl or adult taking part has his or her individual story - a separate memory of his or her experiences. Obviously, it would be impossible to get all these different stories together, all I could do was to give my own personal story in my capacity as the World JOTA Organizer since 1959.

In the text, dealing with the early days of JOTA, I refer to the then Director of the Bureau, Major-General D.C. (Dan) Spry. I personally feel that much of JOTA's success can be attributed to Dan's foresight in those early days and his enthusiasm for the ideas first mooted by Les Mitchell. We all owe him a big vote of thanks.

JOTA could never take place without the cooperation of the amateur radio fraternity. Throughout its history, JOTA has relied on their support, and this support has always been willingly given. We of the Scout Movement owe them a debt of thanks.

I would like to express my personal gratitude to all those National JOTA Organizers who have done so much to make JOTA a success over the years. Without them and their enthusiasm, JOTA would not have been possible at all. I am proud to count them as my friends.

And, while passing out the thanks, I mustn't forget my colleagues at the World Bureau who gave me their encouragement and support over the past 28 years, thus making my job that much easier.

The move to Ottawa

Three years after joining the permanent staff of the (then) Boy Scouts International Bureau in London, I attended the jubilee Jamboree in Sutton Coldfield

CQ Jamboree

near Birmingham. This was my first World Jamboree both as a Scout and as the Administrative Executive for the Bureau. My duties as the latter kept me very busy, and, although I knew that there was an amateur radio station operating from the Jamboree, I had no opportunity of visiting it, with meetings and a side trip to Cambridge to make preparations for the International Conference which was due to follow the Jamboree. In any case, although I had dabbled in building radios as a teenager and had served as an operator during the war, I suppose I really was not keen enough to "make time" to visit the station.

The Cambridge Conference took the (for us) momentous decision to move the Bureau to Ottawa, Canada, and this took effect 1st April, 1958 though I actually sailed on 7th February.

The 1st JOTA 1958

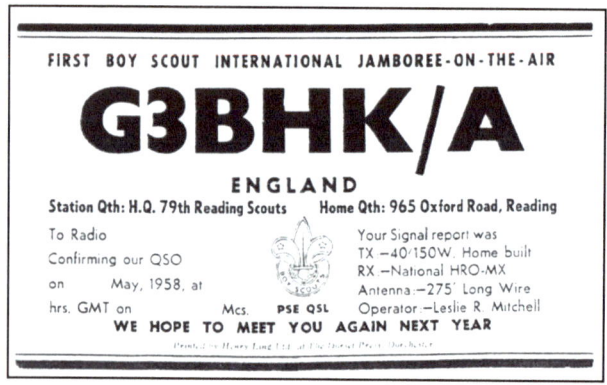

It was soon after my arrival (27th February), that the Bureau issued a circular to all member Associations announcing a "Boy Scout Jamboree-on-the-Air" to be held on 10-11 May, 1958" as announced by the International Scout Club, London." Enquiries were directed to "Hon. Organizer" in Reading, England. This, of course, was Les Mitchell. A similar account was made in "World Scouting" for March, 1958.

The April issue of "World Scouting" repeated the basic information and added that the Bureau's call sign for the event would be VE3RT.

All this came about following receipt of a letter from Les Mitchell asking the Bureau to give the event its blessing and support. I recall that this was discussed at a staff meeting, and the unanimous opinion was that "it wouldn't do any harm to give it a try" and attempt to find a local amateur radio operator to represent the Bureau. If this sounds rather like a lukewarm response, it should be borne in mind that the Bureau continually receives requests to participate in something or other, and it was then, and is still, physically and financially impossible to accept them all.

So Ray Thornton, VE3RT, placed his station and himself at our disposal for three or four hours on Saturday and Sunday, and we, the staff, arranged a rota so that one of us would sit with him during these hours. I don't recall what happened to the others but I do remember that we didn't hear any Scout stations at all during the time that I spent with him. However, my interest in amateur radio was aroused. Subsequently, I found that a cousin of mine in Ottawa, Alf Sheffield, VE3CB, had a station and was, in fact, one of the real old-timers, having experimented with transmitters in the very early days of radio before there were any licences required.

Richard Middelkoop

> "World Scouting" - June, 1958:
>
> RADIO JAMBOREE
>
> Much interest was shown in the Jamboree-on-the-Air but not, unfortunately, by the Clerk of the Weather, for reception conditions during the weekend 10th-11th May, were the worst for many weeks.
>
> In Ottawa, where the International Bureau was invited to operate from Mr. Ray Thornton's station (VE3RT), conditions were so bad that we only could pick up five stations, four of them in Canada and one in the United States. We believe, however, that our calls were heard in other parts of the world. The following letter from "Pat" in Victoria, B.C., proves that the Canadian West Coast heard us:
>
> "I am sending this note for Bill who is blind. He is a short wave fail and belongs to the Boy's Life Radio Club of the Boy Scouts of America in New ' Jersey. He was listening in on your Jamboree over the week-end and picked up VE3RT, Ottawa and GB3BP in Gilwell Park in England."
>
> JAMBOREE-ON-THE-AIR
>
> The Honorary Organizer of the Jamboree, Mr. L. R. Mitchell, reports in a letter to the International Bureau:
>
> "I am very afraid I was unable to organize radio conditions during the Jamboree week-end! I wish I could have done so as these were poor the whole world over.
>
> We were lucky over here as some 20 or more Scout stations took part in about a 100 mile radius of central England and of course we all had a little Jamboree of our own when we couldn't make it overseas!
>
> "Strange as it may seem British Scout Stations did contact Scout Stations in Finland, France, Sweden, Austria, South Africa, Southern Rhodesia, New Zealand, Belgium and Germany. (Also stations with Girl Guides in the room in Japan!) The Canadian stations VE1KK and VE3BLM were heard by the 8th Epsom Scout Receiving Stations over here talking to each other. VE1KK had Scouts in the room. All stations contacted were eager to join in next year and many complained saying they could have organized many more stations if they had heard earlier."
>
> Nothing has as yet been settled about next year's radio Jamboree, but well ahead of the event the propaganda will start and all Scout "hams" hope for a more successful Jamboree-On-the-Air. The Editor of "World Scouting" is anxious to get as many reports as possible on the results and to know if VE3RT was heard, so please drop a line to Boy Scouts International Bureau, 77 Metcalfe St., Ottawa, Ont., Canada.

The June issue of "World Scouting" reported briefly on the event and said that British stations had contacted Scouts in about ten countries and added that "all ... were eager to join in next year". The report went on to say that "nothing has as yet been settled about next year's Jamboree". From these two comments, we can assume that it had already been decided that it was to be an annual event!

I imagine that the Bureau reported on its lack of success to Les and promptly forgot all about it! After all, the Bureau was expanding, we were all, except Dan Spry, trying to get established in a new country with lots and lots to do. So, it was quite understandable that this JOTA idea - which, after all, had not seemed to us to have been at all successful - did not really attract much attention.

CQ Jamboree

I get the job!

Now here again I do not recall the exact date, but my next memory (a very vivid one) is of a staff meeting at which a second letter from Mitchell was discussed. Les wrote that although there had not been too much activity in May 1958, when they first tried to hold a Jamboree-on-the-Air, the attempt had created so much interest that he had been overwhelmed with correspondence. It was apparent that if the event were to continue the organization would be too much for a part-timer; and would the Bureau consider taking it on?

During the ensuing discussion, I can remember saying that I thought the idea had merit and that I agreed with Les' contention that it was a painless and inexpensive way of promoting world brotherhood. Dan Spry was also greatly in favour as was, I believe, our P.R. Director, Lars-Erik Lingstrom. Others were opposed, but when it came to a vote, the "ayes" had it. Dan Spry then asked the question "Now who is going to handle it?" Naturally, we all kept quiet for all of us had more than enough to do, and nobody was looking for more work. Looking round the table, his eye came to rest on me, and he said "Len, you were in the Signals during the war. You must know something about radio. You handle it!"

VE3JAM, with Len Jarrett, operating from Canada on behalf of the Boy Scouts World Bureau in the JOTA in 1959.

Naturally, everybody else was greatly relieved and there was unanimous approval! And that is how I got into JOTA.

Curiously enough, I was never officially given the title of World JOTA Organizer. Until around 1973, I believe, I had always signed JOTA correspondence in my capacity as Director of Administration with, perhaps, the addition of my radio call sign after my name. Then, my secretary, Leyla Bingelli (née Schroeder) decided that since I was, in practice, the World Organizer, I should sign as such, and she started to prepare JOTA correspondence accordingly. It was some time before I woke up to this, and by then no-one had objected -perhaps they did not even notice - so we just carried on, and I started to issue circulars, etc. in this capacity.

Richard Middelkoop

 ## Participation certificates

For the Second JOTA, Dan Spry felt we should issue some sort of participation certificate - probably at Les Mitchell's instigation. Finances at the Bureau were extremely tight at the time, the budget was already heavily overspent, so we had to do it "on the cheap". We found a Scouter who had his own hand printing machine at home, and I can recall spending several evenings with this Scouter in his basement helping him to print the cards. There were probably only 500 or so in those days so that it was not a big job. For the first three JOTA's, Dan Spry personally signed each card, (these must be collector's items now!) but after that, the job became too big. It is interesting to note that these participation certificates were sent only to "those sending reports of activity to the Bureau". It seems that, even in those early days, we had difficulty in getting people to send reports.

This first card was designed by a local volunteer as were, I believe, the next two. It was not until around 1961 that we started to "borrow" artwork from other JOTA organizers (notably Australia for a year or so, I believe). Later on, we started to ask various National Organizers to "volunteer" artwork.

The quantity of participation certificates printed by the Bureau serves as a good indication of the growth of JOTA. The number started at 500 copies of the first card produced and reached 100,000 by 1981, while, in addition, several countries and at least one region (Asia-Pacific) printed their own.

The World Scout Bureau since only recently has a complete set of these cards, thanks to several volunteers who donated them.

The 2nd JOTA 1959

The first JOTA had been held in May, 1958, but encountered problems with various radio contests being held at the same time. Since we were newcomers, we decided to change the timing and after much searching, Les suggested the third weekend in October as being relatively free of other events. And there, with but one or two exceptions, we have stayed ever since. The event soon became, as "World Scouting" reported "part of the regular Scouting calendar in many countries".

CQ Jamboree

For the Second JOTA, held over the weekend of 24-25 October, 1959, VE3RT was not available so the Bureau used the facilities of Bert Coy, VE3GI, and the special call sign of VE3JAM. Once again, the staff shared the watch keeping duties. Again, I cannot recall if we talked to any other Scout stations. A report was not issued in those days and all correspondence has since been destroyed. However, I assume that we made some contacts, for the December, 1959, issue of "World Scouting" stated that "it can now be taken for granted that the Jamboree-on-the-Air is here to stay" for incoming reports showed that there were "a comparatively great number of Scout stations" in operation despite the fact that "information (about JOTA) had not been spread as widely as could be desired".

"World Scouting" - December, 1959:

SCOUTS-on-the-AIR

It can now be taken for granted that the Jamboree-on-the-Air is here to stay. This year it was held on October 24th-25th, and, although still far from perfect, it showed such encouraging results that it will be repeated in 1960.

A comparatively great number of Scout stations seem to have been in operation, and many contacts were made, but it still appears that transatlantic contacts were rather scarce. Unfortunately, a radio amateur contest was going on at the same time as the Jamboree and, on occasions, it made radio telephony traffic quite difficult. It is also evident that information about the radio Jamboree had not been spread as widely as could be desired, in spite of all the efforts of the International Bureau.

Reports to the International Bureau indicate that some Scoutmasters have made good use of the "Scout radio weekend" for the benefit of their troops. Here is an extract from a letter, written by the Scout-master of 3rd Richmond Hill Group, Ontario, Canada, which shows what can be done:

"Being very "brotherhood conscious" we thought this event would be a very good way of demonstrating the meaning of Scout brotherhood in a practical manner. The 48 hours were split into two hour watches, each of four patrols rotating with two boys on watch at a time. This was for the purpose of keeping "wireless watch" so that all possible advantage was taken to listen to other Scouts taking part.

At our troop Headquarters for the weekend there were two communications receivers at the troop's disposal. Apart from the watches, a programme of games and Scouting was organised including cooking on Coleman stoves. During the weekend boys were taken out in pairs to different amateur radio stations where they had the opportunity of speaking to Scouts from parts known and unknown. One of the Patrol Leaders was lucky enough to make contact with the International Bureau in Ottawa, whose special call letters for the occasion were VE3JAM. Two boys from another patrol made contact with a troop in England.

The weekend was made quite exciting by the fact that a contest was made up for patrol points; and naturally, VE3JAM was good for bonus points, as were contacts from the furthest points of contact with other Scouts. All boys got considerable practice at log keeping both at the troop headquarters and at amateur stations. In all, 44 Scout contacts were made, including most ranks from Tenderfoot to District Commissioner. We endeavour to make our signalling more interesting by using short wave radio and eventually hope to have a troop station. To get to this point, a boy must of course, be able to send and receive code at a speed of 10 words per minute and know a certain amount of theory. In this manner the troop could also render the community some service in time of emergency."

Richard Middelkoop

The 3rd JOTA 1960

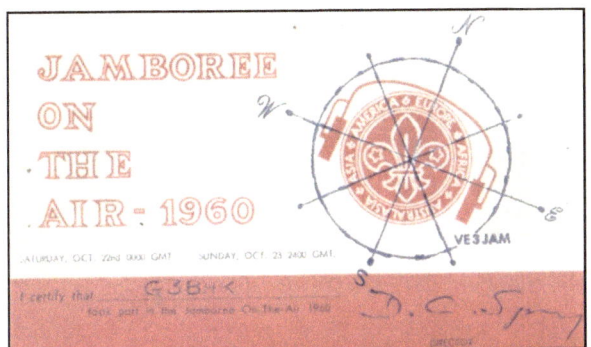

During the third JOTA, held on 22-23 October, 1960, the local radio club, prodded by Ray Thornton and Alf Sheffield, became involved as did the Army Signal Corps. The call sign VE3JAM was again used and the Army gave permission to use Connaught Ranges, a camp just outside Ottawa, where the Signal Corps erected antennas "as an exercise". The equipment was superb - I believe we had three transmitters operating simultaneously, each running the maximum legal output. Results fully justified this lavish organization. Canadian Scouts had carried out massive publicity and, as a result, nearly 400 Canadian stations took part. I think VE3JAM spoke to almost every one. Certainly we were on the go for the full 48 hours and, according to the November issue of "World Scouting", VE3JAM made over 400 contacts in 23 countries.

Other countries reported increased participation too, and so, for the first time, the Bureau issued a report, albeit a very slim one by present standards. Comments received were summarized and grouped by continent - separate reports by country did not start for another two years.

In Britain, the "Short Wave Magazine" reported on the event and mentioned that Scout David Sochachewsky of London had just received his licence, having been introduced to amateur radio at the first JOTA in May, 1958. Since then many others have become involved in amateur radio as a result of JOTA.

At about this time, some National Scout Associations started to install permanent amateur radio stations. The January, 1961, issue of "World Scouting" reports DU1BSP in the Philippines and YV5ARS in Venezuela, while remarking that K2BFW in the USA and XE1EW in Mexico had been operating for some time. It would not be long before the Bureau itself and other National Associations followed suit.

For me, the third JOTA was memorable, because it was then that I decided to get my own licence, for I felt a little left out of things listening to the "ham talk" during the weekend, and decided that "if you can't beat them - join them". So, in November, 1960, I constructed a Heathkit AR3 receiver, stuck up an antenna on my apartment roof and started to listen to W1AW's practice C.W. sessions and to study technical manuals. The next year, I became the proud owner of the call VE3EWE (perfect for C.W.) and immediately ordered and constructed a Heathkit DX60 transmitter. But when I started to transmit, all my neighbours objected, for not knowing any better, I had laid my antenna on the roof (it had to be kept out of sight) across the master TV feeder. Operation had to be restricted to non-TV hours until I solved the whole problem by moving to a house with a garden.

CQ Jamboree

A Permanent Bureau station

Soon after this we decided that, since the Bureau now had a licensed amateur on its staff, it should have a permanent radio station. The problem was money because the Bureau still didn't have any funds to spare. One day, I happened to be reading a radio magazine and noticed an advertisement claiming that "Anyone can build a Heathkit". So I wrote to the advertiser, Daystrom Ltd., suggesting that it would be good publicity for them to have a "World" station using their equipment, especially if it were to be constructed by Scouts. I did not hold out much hope of success but then unexpectedly I got a call from Jack Baldwin, VE3BS, the then President of Daystrom Canada, saying that he was coming to Ottawa and would like to discuss the matter. He came and was impressed with our ideas and agreed to present us with all the equipment we were likely to need.

Of course, it was about ten times the size of similar modern equipment and looked very impressive when completed. It could handle both AM and CW, and, also, the newfangled SSB which was just coming into amateur use. It was assembled by members of a local Rover Crew under my supervision and needed only minor adjustment and tuning before it could be put "on the air".

Incidentally, Jack Baldwin was a very good friend of Scouting and, due to his interest, Heathkit Canada subsequently produced a cheap transistor radio kit especially for Scouts. Unfortunately, its price could not compete with that of the Japanese imports which came on the market about the same time and so it was soon discontinued. Nevertheless, it was a good set, and I still use one in my kitchen.

World JOTA Organizer Len Jarrett explains the radio contacts to a group of Girl Scouts visiting the World Scout Bureau station VE3WSB in 1961.

We managed to find funds for a tower and a tri-band beam, and, with the aid of Steve Chishohn, VE3ATU, then a Captain in the Signal Corps and sundry other friends, we managed to erect it on the "hut" holding the elevator machinery on the roof of the Commonwealth Building where the Bureau's offices were located. The antenna was about 110 feet above ground level. Since at that time, the height of buildings in the city of Ottawa could not exceed that of Parliament, we could proudly claim to have the highest antenna in the city.

Richard Middelkoop

VE3WSB makes its debut

On February 22, 1961, VE3WSB was officially opened by the Deputy Minister of External Affairs in the presence of a number of dignitaries including the Radio Inspector and the Canadian Director of American Radio Relay League. Dan Spry was in the Bahamas at the time, and we arranged that he, with some other stations, would appear "on the air" at the right time to pass greetings. Everything worked well to my great relief, so well, in fact, that the radio experts accused us of having pre-recorded the whole thing.

The following October, VE3WSB started operation on a regular schedule which included CW practice transmissions of Scout news on Friday evenings for an hour. This lasted six months until we transmitted a request for feedback to see how we were doing. Since we did not get one reply, the CW sessions came to a rapid end, although our scheduled operation continued. The local amateur radio club used VE3WSB's shack for its beginners' courses for several years too.

The 4th JOTA 1961

The fourth JOTA, in 1961, is notable for the following report received from Japan: "I dearly present to you the report of all time - readability - nil, strength - nil." Twenty-two National Organizers known to exist. World report issued for the first time.

Great willingness to co-operate among the amateur radio fraternity: "they only have to be asked". More than 50 references to the event in Scout magazines were counted. Many JOTA stations appeared on TV and national radio.

The new Baden-Powell House in London hosted JOTA station GB3BPH. The Bureau's Regional Office in Mexico City operated for the first time with XE1ASM.

The 4th Camden Group in New South Wales, Australia taking part in the 4th JOTA with VK2ADA.

The 5th JOTA 1962

A special JOTA Badge was produced from Les Mitchell's design and a leaflet, "Getting the Most from JOTA" was put together in English. It subsequently came out in many other languages. Sixty-three countries took part.

The Australian Scout Leader magazine of October 1962 headlined: "Any Scout can participate in this Jamboree!"

Anybody who has taken part once, wants to do so again, said the World JOTA Report.

The 6th JOTA 1963

The new Canadian Scout H.Q. was completed on the outskirts of Ottawa in 1963, and VE3WSB started to use that for JOTA. There was tremendous enthusiasm for JOTA among Canadian Scouts and each year there were around 400 Scout stations in operation. This was reflected in the number of visitors to VE3WSB. The cafeteria where the three stations were installed was packed throughout the weekend - sometimes even at night. Manufacturers seemed to fall over themselves to lend us the most modern equipment, while we were besieged by the press, radio and TV. For the Bureau, this was really the heyday of JOTA. VE3WSB continued to use the Canadian Scout H.Q. for JOTA for the next three events. Visitors still packed the room and our station appeared every year on TV and radio and in the press.
In total 53 of our 80 member Associations were active in JOTA.

In South-Africa, at 24th Pretoria Sea Scouts, "the boys could not be lured from the equipment even with the offer of a swim".

A 14 Watt portable station operated from Brownsea Island, UK, by the 1st Oakdale troop in pouring rain.

Richard Middelkoop

Scouts in Huddersfield, United Kingdom having fun in the 6th JOTA with GB3CMS.

The 7th JOTA 1964

The World JOTA Report presents an overview per country for the first time, and no longer a summary per region.

ZL2BAL claims highest Scout-built tower in the world - 100 feet of bamboo and mauka (a small tree).

Mexico reports to have obtained a large number of new Scout leaders from the radio amateur ranks.

Zambia took part for the first time with 3 stations and Scouts hope to get their own station soon with the help of the local police.

Iran formed a National JOTA Committee and aired 6 stations. They mention: "the participation of Girls Scouts proved very helpful and effective" and recommend joint activities.

In Singapore, 9M4SJ had a marathon QSO with Scouts in Ceylon: they exchanged songs for over an hour!

Big is beautiful…. in 1964 the amateur radio equipment was sometimes larger than the Scouts, like here at this JOTA station in Peru.

CQ Jamboree

The 9 Scout groups in Lourenco Marques, the capital of Mozambique joined together at CR7BS and talked to 43 Scout groups in South Africa.

Scouts in Pakistan operated for the first time with a station of the Signal Battalion in Dacca and contacted many stations using Morse Code.

The operator at 5Z4KSA in Kenya was recalled to England, but the Scouts managed to find a replacement the very evening before JOTA.

The 8th JOTA 1965

An Indian troop, not being able to obtain a transmitter, set up a listening station and held an investiture. The leader reported: "In past ceremonies I had found it hard to get the Scouts to believe in the existence of World Brotherhood. This time it was no problem, and the investiture was so much more meaningful."

In Colombia, a patrol of 8 visited an amateur radio station; when they left they were 10: the 2 sons of the operator joined the troop.

6Y5RA in Kingston, Jamaica calling…

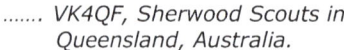

……. VK4QF, Sherwood Scouts in Queensland, Australia.

Richard Middelkoop

The 9th JOTA 1966

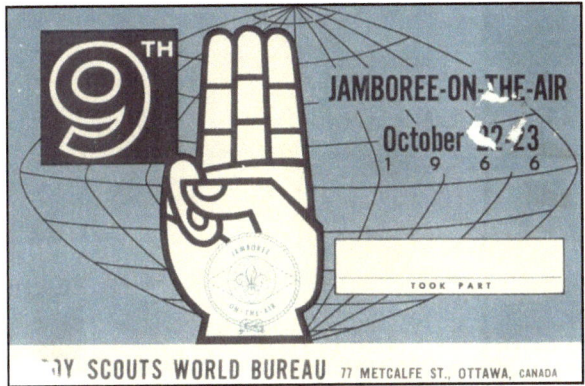

Ideal conditions reported, but JOTA clashed with CQ amateur radio contest, despite our early notification of dates. Discussions with CQ Magazine and ARRL to try to avoid recurrence.

Over 170 reports received with tremendous improvements in organization. An appendix to the World Report with the detailed JOTA organization schedule from Norway as an example to others.

A staggering 128 stations in South Africa claiming a "world record" of having 1 station for every 13 Scouts.

A model camp was held in Montevideo, Uruguay. CX4AAD placed speakers outside so that visitors in the exhibition could listen to the radio contacts.

4X4TP operated for about 18 hours from the Scout HQ in Tel Aviv.

A massive 450 stations are active in Australia. Undoubtedly, the enthusiasm is attributed to the organization that has been built up by NJO Noel Lynch over the years; there are organizing committees at every level of the Scout Association.

The 1st Sorumsand Scouts in Norway on the air for the 9th JOTA with LA8RG.

CQ Jamboree

The 10th JOTA 1967

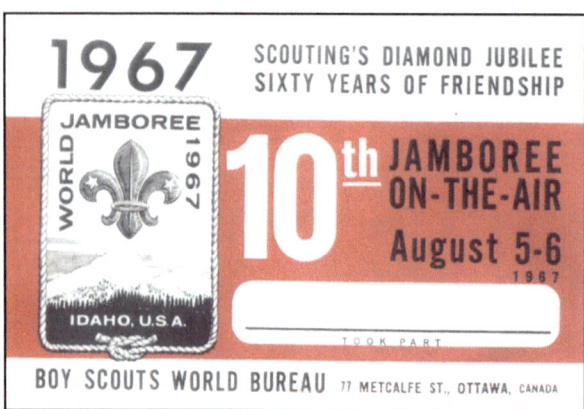

In 1967 the World Jamboree was held in Idaho, USA and the host organization had arranged a special radio station with the call of K7WSJ. It was agreed to hold JOTA over the weekend of 5-6 August for there were many special "link" camps with radio's set up around the world, notably on Brownsea Island and at Mafeking. For the first time, the World Bureau did not have its own JOTA station in operation. Instead, it used K7WSJ. However, the experiment was not popular, and this was the only year that we tried a date other than a weekend in October.

K7WSJ at the World Jamboree.

An NJO address list appears in the World Report for the first time and lists 25 National Organizers.

Also, this year, the World Conference decided to move the World Bureau to Switzerland, making the 10th JOTA the last one for the Bureau in Canada. We dismantled the permanent station and donated the equipment to the Rover Crew that had helped to construct it. Subsequently, they used it to establish a permanent station at the Canadian Scout H.Q., using the call sign of VE3SHQ.

In Sutton Coldfield, UK, the station GB3GP (originally at the 1957 World Jamboree, JOTA's birthplace) was revived by one of its original operators, Tom Douglas.

Richard Middelkoop

The 11th JOTA 1968

The Bureau went to Geneva and, in temporary offices, used the facilities of the International Telecommunications Union (ITU) Amateur Radio Club and their rare call sign of 4UIITU for the JOTA's of 1968 and 1969. The equipment and location were superb. The only problem was that, because the call sign was so unique, we were besieged by non-JOTA stations all the time and found it difficult to carry out our proper role. First JOTA "Aeronautical Mobile" reported by South Africa. World Report the biggest yet.

The 12th JOTA 1969

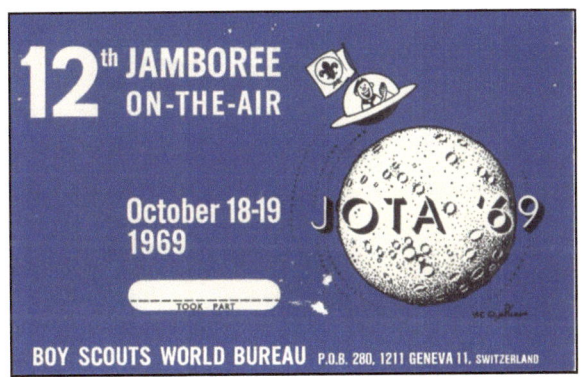

4UIITU was used again and made nearly 600 contacts in 59 countries during the 48 hours it operated. Conditions were superb. Les says "the best year yet. The event is now standing firmly on its own feet and I really feel that we are making it work for us".

"Radio-Scouting" starts to grow. The third full weekend in October has been established, by mutual agreement with Amateur Radio Associations and magazines, as the JOTA weekend.

"For young people, their fellow members in the World Brotherhood of Scouting became real through JOTA", says the preface to the World Report. "A station near the artic circle tells Scouts in Ontario, Canada, about polar bears visiting the station.

Austrian Girl-Scouts with their enormous station OE9IM in Bregenz.

CQ Jamboree

Scouts in Iceland chat about the Beatles with a Liverpool group. Scouts in Singapore exchange Scout songs with Scouts in Ecuador, India and Australia. A Dutch group invites the Icelandic "Jokers" group at Reykjavik to camp with them next summer".

HB9S appears

It was not until late 1970, when the World Bureau was able to move to its permanent location in a building owned by Geneva Scout Foundation, that it was possible for it to again have a permanent station.

Luckily the Bureau was involved in the early planning of the building and was able to arrange for the necessary fittings on the roof for the installation of an antenna tower, and, also, for the cables to run inside down to the "shack" on the first floor. In the meantime, I had obtained a Swiss licence for the office (we had to form a club first). We had hoped to obtain HB9WSB but were informed that this was not possible as calls were allocated in sequence, and they had only reached the "A's"; my own call was HB9AMS. However, the PTT in Berne were most cooperative and told us that the call HB9S was available if we wanted it. Of course, we said "Yes, please" without hesitation.

Equipment was, naturally a problem, and, for a while, HB9S used my equipment. However, a letter to the Boy Scouts of Nippon was answered with an offer to equip a station "in memory of the late 'Willie' Padolina", the Bureau's executive in the Asia-Pacific Region, who had died suddenly a month or so earlier. We gratefully accepted and purchased Japanese equipment where possible. The station was formally inaugurated on 22 February, 1971 - the same time as the new offices were officially opened.

Unfortunately, the location - between a streetcar line and the hospital - was not exactly ideal, but we managed to take part in the European Scout Net on Saturday mornings whenever my duties permitted.

HM King Carl Gustav of Sweden (centre) visits HB9S in 1978, accompanied by Len Jarrett (right).

Richard Middelkoop

The 13th JOTA 1970

For the 13th and subsequent JOTA's, whenever we elected to operate HB9S from its home base, we moved the equipment into the reception area where there was space for visitors. In addition to our permanent beam antenna, we tried out various wire and vertical antennas for the lower frequencies and added a second station, for we had a second transceiver and had prudently provided a second coaxial feeder to the roof. However, 80 meter operation was never really successful as there was not room on the roof for a full-size wire antenna and trap antennas always seemed to produce irate, TV watching, neighbours on our doorstep. In any case, it was virtually impossible to operate two stations in the close quarters of our reception room. This was for technical reasons and not because we were overwhelmed with visitors. When we operated JOTA from Geneva, we never received anywhere near the number of visitors that we had become accustomed to in Ottawa.

The JOTA leaflet is now available in eight languages. An impressive increase in the number of "Scout-designed or printed" QSL cards noted.

The 14th JOTA 1971

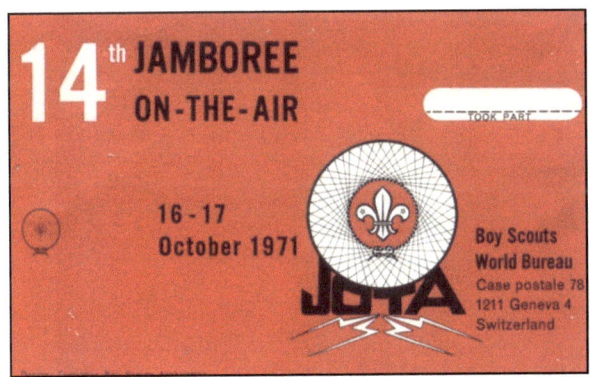

Experiment of starting at midnight local time seems a success in overcoming the school and work problems for those countries in the Asia-Pacific Region. Eighty-eight countries participated.

A Norwegian Guide was "thrilled to death" when she realized that what she said in her school English had been fully understood by the Scouts in the USA.

In Botswana, A2CAH operated from Khale with 200 Scouts. They were able to exchange greetings with Mafikeng and even as far apart as Brownsea Island.

Rhodesia had one station in each province, whilst there were 4 stations in total in Panama.

CQ Jamboree

In The Netherlands, a portable station adds "/A" to its call sign, so that PA0JOT became most appropriately PA0JOT/A.

VIP guests get involved in the JOTA: the Minister of Communications performs the 14th JOTA opening for the Netherlands Antilles.

The 15th JOTA 1972

HB9S ventures to the top of Mount Chasseron - 1608 meters above sea level - to get away from the static which plagued us in Geneva, and encounters winds of 120 kph and heavy snow, thus forcing the station to close early to avoid the operators being marooned. A photograph which appeared in the JOTA report one year showed us evacuating the station, and has been likened to the retreat from Moscow.

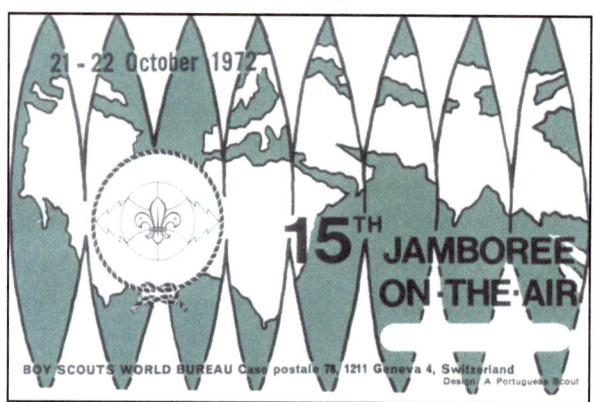

Eighteen-year-old Siri Fuglesang, from Oslo, Norway sums up in the World Report. We did not know then that she was to become LA2SR herself and the wife of a well-known Radio-Scouter, Tom-Victor Segalstad, LA4LN. Siri writes: "some reports describe long contacts with foreign countries, some of which are bound to end up with letters- and badge exchanges. Others

This is TI2FGS calling from San José, Costa Rica….

26

tell about contacts with rare countries and islands. All of them convey the enthusiasm shown by Scouts and Guides alike".

Scouts in Angola offered a special first day cover with a JOTA postmark.

In The Netherlands a Scout contest was held, to get the most points by adding up the troop number of the Scout troops contacted by radio.

The 16th JOTA 1973

HB9S on Mount Chasseron again. Weather is a little better but winds still around 100 kph. Eighty-nine countries participated. A "break-through" year for Radio-Scouting in Norway. Fox-hunting receivers, etc., designed and constructed.

The first JOTA handbook published with the help of the Commemorative Fund of the Japan Expo'70.

The European Scout Net, along with other national nets, appears on the scene. HB9S acts as net control each Saturday morning on the 20 m band. Len Jarrett receives the Bronze Wolf.

The 17th JOTA 1974

World Report repeats the "basic recipe for JOTA success", first published in 1964: 1. Appoint a National Organizer, preferably a "ham". 2. Give adequate publicity. 3. Plan ahead; do not leave everything to the last moment.

At HB9S it was difficult to find a spot anywhere on our authorized frequencies which was not occupied by JOTA stations within Europe and our time was fully occupied throughout the entire weekend.

Les, G3BHK, operates the British HQ station from the facilities of the Science Research Council.

CQ Jamboree

The 18th JOTA 1975

A milestone for Radio-Scouting as a result of the magnificent exhibit at the World Scout Jamboree in Norway. Three thousand five hundred electronic kits constructed; Sixteen-hundred Scouts experienced fox-hunting using Scout-constructed receivers. First World JOTA Conference held with 60 delegates from 22 different countries.

The Netherlands gets permission for Scouts to speak directly over radio, starting a Radio-Scouting boom in that country.

The 19th JOTA 1976

"Terrible, the worst in 19 years of JOTA", said the World Report. This was supposed to be "Scout Communications Year", but no-one had thought to tell Mother Nature.

Richard Middelkoop gets introduced to the JOTA for the first time, at the St. Stanislaus Scoutinggroup in Culemborg, The Netherlands.

Our largest Scout Association, the Boy Scouts of America, was active with, for the first time, over 1000 stations; a wonderful achievement.

The originators of the wider "Radio-Scouting" programme, our friends from Norway, did not rest on their laurels, but they are fast being challenged by The Netherlands, while several other countries are coming fast behind. More are beginning to realize that that the activity offers something of interest to everybody within the framework of the normal Scout programme.

Radio Scouting has come a long way since Les Mitchell first thought of the idea of having an annual get-together "on the air". The Chief Scout of the UK recognised Les' contributions and on St. Georges Day 1976 awarded him the Silver Wolf.

Richard Middelkoop

The 20th JOTA 1977

For the first time since the event started, the World Bureau did not have its own station on the air. I had felt for a long time that I should see something of the REAL JOTA at the troop level away from the rarefied "H.Q." aura.

A hint to Pieter Kramer, National Organizer for The Netherlands, brought an invitation to visit them for the 20th JOTA weekend in 1977. So off we (my wife and I) went to The Netherlands for a wonderful weekend. We visited no less than 20 stations and got all sorts of new ideas. It was a real recharging of my JOTA batteries, and I am most grateful to all the wonderful friends that I met and particularly to Pieter and Rimke, his wife, for their generous hospitality. Seventy-nine countries with about 6,000 stations, took part.

An impressive pioneering object at PA0TOI/A, The Netherlands.

The 21st JOTA 1978

Inspired by my experiences in The Netherlands, we decided to commemorate the 21st JOTA (its coming of age) by holding an International Camp at the Geneva Scouts' campsite at Satigny, near Geneva, and inviting Swiss, French, Canadian and

USA troops. The latter were drawn from the troops set up by the USA residents in Geneva while the Canadian Scouts came all the way

Sorek Scout group in kibbutz Harel, Israel enjoying the 21st JOTA with 4Z4QE.

CQ Jamboree

from Lahr, Germany. In total 150 Scouts attended. All sorts of "radio" activities were included, as well as several radio stations and SSTV or RTTY stations. The camp proved to be extremely popular and was a lot of fun. Things to remember: the difficulty of getting pioneering poles and our horror at seeing the nice curly birch poles that eventually arrived, the fire alarm which went off accidentally in the middle of the night (and no one knew where the cut off switch was), the thrill at seeing the first SSTV CQ answered.

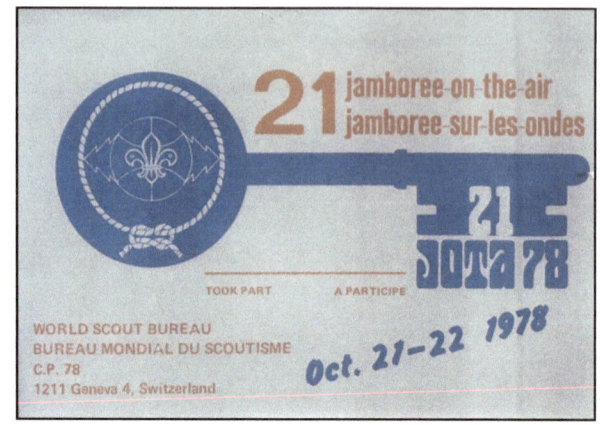

Ninety-two "radio" countries including 64 full members of the World Organization participated in JOTA.

Les Mitchell is awarded the Bronze Wolf, the only recognition of the World Organization of the Scout Movement, in December 1978.

The 22nd JOTA 1979

By universal demand, we again held an International Camp at Satigny with Swiss, French and American Scouts and, most popular of all, a French Girl Guide unit.

Radio conditions were excellent and we contacted 205 Scout stations in 38 countries, covering all continents.

We felt, however, that it would be a mistake to make these camps a regular feature. Instead, we tried to persuade the local Swiss and USA troops to set up their own, but to no avail.

The 23rd JOTA 1980

Early in 1980, a casual comment in a letter from Les Mitchell about "JOTA Oldtimers" gave me the idea that, perhaps, the World Scout Bureau could operate a JOTA station from the U.K. at least once. Les took up the idea with enthusiasm and we ended up near Datchet for the 23rd JOTA. We used the call sign GB2WSB and had a team of operators with a combined JOTA experience of over 100 years. I

Richard Middelkoop

think that we did more reminiscing than operating.

Nigeria claims a 240-foot mast, but it is doubtful that it is Scout-constructed. Seventy-four countries listed as being active including, for the first time, Antarctica.

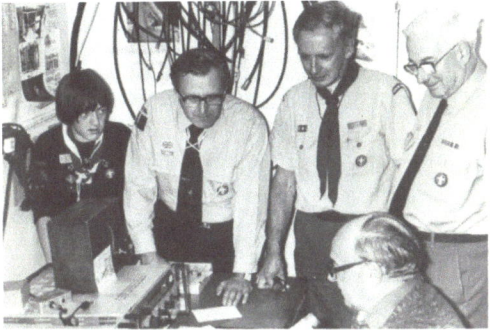

The founding fathers of JOTA, Les Mitchell, right, and Len Jarrett, standing next to him, in the 23rd JOTA with World Scout Bureau station GB2WSB, operating from the United Kingdom this year.

Decision to resign

Early in 1981, I decided to resign as Director of Administration for the World Scout Bureau and to return to Canada. I agreed to stay on as World JOTA Organizer for the time being, and, as it happened, the Bureau asked me to accept part-time employment as well. This allowed me to return to Geneva from time to time to operate HB9S during JOTA.

The 24th JOTA 1981

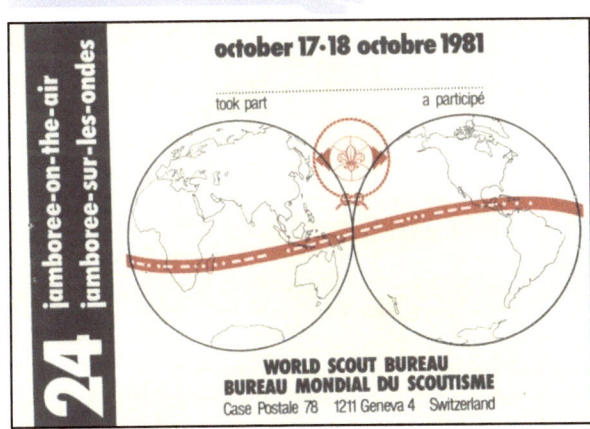

A letter from Poland lists 81 call signs of "Scout" stations taking part in JOTA. Seventy-eight "radio" countries participated this year, and the World Report challenges readers to have 100 countries in 1982 - the 25th anniversary of JOTA and the 75th anniversary of Scouting. (25+75=100).

HB9S contacts GB2BPH, operated by Les at a meeting of International Commissioners. WOSM Secretary General Laszlo Nagy was present and could reassure himself that HB9S really works.

The 25th JOTA 1982

The World Report this year lists 98 countries taking part, but it subsequently turned out that that there were four more so that our goal of 100 countries was reached and even surpassed. A breakthrough in the U.K.: exhibition stations (those with GB call) may allow Scouts to speak, but only to other GB stations. We hope it is just the thin edge of the wedge.

The 26th JOTA 1983

Propagation "extremely poor". Home computers appear in strength for the first time on RTTY and CW as well as logging. This makes it easier for the average Scout to enjoy a contact by CW. Quite a number of contacts were made using the Amateur Satellite OSCAR 10.

National Organizers suffer from the failure to send in reports of the activity. One says: "300 groups took the trouble to obtain a special call sign, but less than 25%

"Hi, I am Paolo form Manila…." DU1BSP, Boy Scouts of the Philippines in action for the 25th JOTA.

bothered to report. When radio conditions are poor, everybody tries to avoid letting us know how badly they have done...."

GB3RSS from Yorkshire, UK, sums up in the World Report as having taken part in every JOTA so far with the same call sign. Des Walker, G3JWN, writes a 2-page story on their success.

Radio-Scouting takes another step forward with the "Elektron" exhibit at the World Scout Jamboree in Alberta, Canada, including radio station VE6WSJ. The antenna array, in particular, was most impressive. The station kept a daily schedule with The Netherlands where the contingent news was recorded on a telephone answering machine at the National Office, for parents to dial in to.

Paul Martin, EI2CA, the National JOTA Organizer for Ireland, held a presentation on JOTA and Radio-Scouting at the World Scout Conference in Dearborn, USA, which was very well received by the 500 leaders present from 80 different countries.

The 27th JOTA 1984

Conditions were worse than the previous year. During my absence, HB9S's tower had almost fallen down, and we had to operate with a temporary dipole. Ninety-two "radio" countries listed as taking part.

A European JOTA Organizers Conference had been held in The Netherlands in May. A questionnaire was subsequently sent to all countries. Replies from 47 printed in the World Report - very informative.

P29JOA in Papua New Guinea organizes a quiz for 300 Scouts.

In Australia, Noel Lynch, VK4BNL, resigns, after 19 years as National JOTA Organizer, leaving an impressive JOTA organization to his successor.

CQ Jamboree

The 28th JOTA 1985

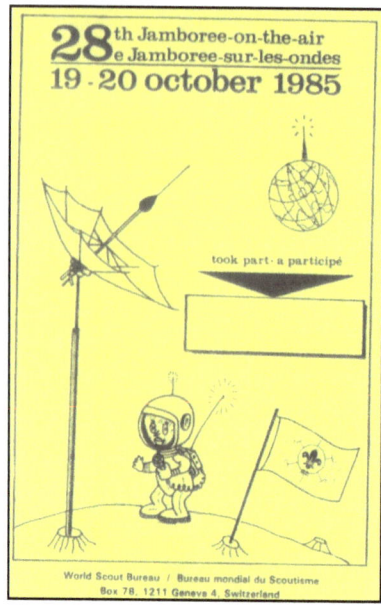

Although the HB9S's tower had been made safe again, the antenna cable had still not been repaired, and at the suggestion of Swiss Organizer, Yves Margot, HB9AOF, we decided to move out to Satigny Scout Camp for the weekend where Yves and some of his Scouts erected antennas. Operation was very successful.

Yves offers to operate HB9S during the year, and, in particular, for the European Scout Net on Saturday mornings as often as possible. I gladly accept and advise the Swiss authorities that Yves is now responsible for the station.

The World Report mentions unofficial "Scout" stations taking part from Poland, Czechoslovakia and Yugoslavia.

Queen Ingrid, the Queen Mother, opens JOTA in Denmark; H.R.H. Prince Claus does the same in The Netherlands. JOTA is now a "royal" event. Les Mitchell writes in the UK report: "….it is better to have a few really friendly, interesting and relaxed contacts than a hundred quick ones. On a World Scout Jamboree you do not go rushing around the site saying "Hello – Goodbye" to every Scout either……."

The 29th JOTA 1986

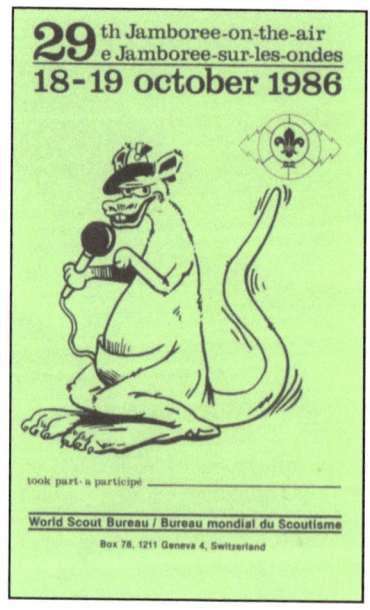

For me the 29th JOTA was memorable because for the first time ever I operated a "normal" JOTA station, that is, not one that is always in great demand, and not an H.Q. station. It was something I should have done years earlier.

The 29th JOTA stands out in my memory for another reason - the great increase in the number of USA Scout stations "on the air", and the first complete report on JOTA activity ever received from that country, thanks to a new and enthusiastic "Radio Committee".

Oman joined in for the first time, while the Italian Scouts activated the Vatican station HV1CN. Propagation was rather patchy, but there were indications that the new sun spot cycle was under way.

Both the UK and USA reports stressed the need for planning for JOTA. A total of 81 countries took part.

Richard Middelkoop

The 30th JOTA 1987

HB9S operates again, with new equipment, from Satigny Scout Camp and this year Yves had with him two guest operators - Richard Middelkoop, PA3BAR, and Duncan Wheelhouse, G8TRP, as well as local Swiss operators. I myself operated VE3MYF for a short time and logged about six JOTA stations in three countries.

The report shows that 85 countries participated and reports came in from 39 of them (46%), which must be quite a record.

There was some good news from the UK too, for it appears that a form of Student License may be introduced there, and that Scouting would be represented on the Committee.

In Dubai amateur radio is not permitted, but Alan G3WNS mounted a listening station with the 2nd Dubai cub pack.

The Scout Association in Barbados celebrated their 75th anniversary with 8P75BBS.

AX2SWJ operated from the World Scout Jamboree in Australia at the start of 1988, with outstanding success.

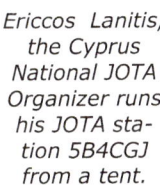

Ericcos Lanitis, the Cyprus National JOTA Organizer runs his JOTA station 5B4CGJ from a tent.

CQ Jamboree

ANOTHER THIRTY YEARS by Richard Middelkoop

Taking over from an experienced World JOTA Organizer as Len Jarrett was not an easy thing to do. In fact, we needed two persons for that. Henceforth, Yves Margot, HB9AOF continued to look after the World Scout Bureau's own amateur radio station HB9S and all technical things needed for that. He took over the licence from Len. It became my task to edit the annual World JOTA Report and write the information circulars for the National Scout Associations. Luckily, I had some experience with this, as I had served several years as the editor of the JOTA news bulletins in The Netherlands. The Dutch national Radio-Scouting working group of Pieter Kramer, PA3BIV, had been an excellent learning school to me. As I am working in a volunteer capacity, this meant working at a distance from Geneva. Similar to what Len had done while he was working from Canada. So, to get to know the regular World Scout Bureau staff was of utmost importance.

In those early years, the director of World Events, Jean Cassaigneau, was my prime point of contact. Jean made sure the JOTA event got the resources it needed and took care of things at the Geneva office. To me, the secretary of the World Events unit was just as important. Jacqueline Paschoud handled al the JOTA correspondence in a very professional way and took care of the printing of the World JOTA Report. She was also part of the jury for competitions we had for reports and the annual logo. And to finish it off, Jacqueline cooked many meals for us whilst we were operating HB9S during JOTA.

In those days, I wrote the JOTA report by hand, my XYL Miriam typed it on a type writer, I cut all photos by hand to fit onto a page and then sent the camera-ready copy to Geneva in a big package. How different from today.

The 31st JOTA, 1988

Radio propagation conditions were excellent this year. Many long distance contacts were made.

A suggestion was received from France, promoting the use of Esperanto to communicate during JOTA. Increased use of packet radio was noted.

The Danish Minister of Communications stressed the importance of JOTA to Scouts in isolated areas and The Netherlands reported radio interference with electronics in a water tower, where suddenly the meters showed empty.

In New-Zealand a JOTA station assisted in handling an emergency involving a boat which overturned on a large river.

The 2nd European Radio-Scouting seminar is held in May in Satigny, Switzerland with participation of nearly all European JOTA organizers; HB9S operates from Satigny during the seminar. Len Jarrett writes his last World JOTA Report.

The 32nd JOTA 1989

Solar flares occurred just before the JOTA weekend caused problems with long-distance communication. Aurora (the Northern Light) was visible as far south as France. The bad radio conditions prompted many participants to start side activities like electronic-kit building.

In Australia Scouts in the outback were taking part in JOTA as well; the radio networks of the Royal Flying Doctors Service, the National Telephone System and the School of the Air were all connected to the amateur radio network. And some satellite channels were made available to the Scouts by AUSSAT.

Les Mitchell, the JOTA originator, and his wife visited several JOTA stations in The Netherlands for which they drove nearly a thousand miles. "A thousand miles of friendship", Les concluded.

The Polish amateur radio organization celebrates its 60th anniversary. Amateur radio was introduced in Poland in 1922 by ...Scouts, making the first contacts with a spark transmitter.

From Sri Lanka blind Scouts went on the air with Morse code and a transceiver with voice indicators for various functions.

In Wales a cub Scout asked his radio operator to send the word "Supercalifragilisticexpealidocious" in Morse code. The receiving station, however, could not pronounce it.

The 33rd JOTA 1990

The newly recognized Scout organizations in Hungary and Czechoslovakia went on the air. The Scout station FF1SDF at the World Scout Conference in Paris in July had provoked their interest. For the first time Scouts from Turkey took part also with TA1KA from Istanbul. The National TV news covered the event and their report even included a video tape.

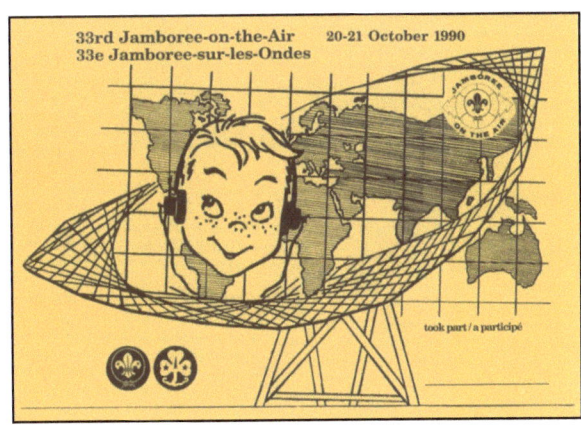

The German JOTA organizer wanted to transmit a puzzle game, but was puzzled himself when his equipment transmitted smoke signals instead.

In Jamaica the National station was swamped with cub Scouts suddenly and the JOTA organizer found himself "nursemaiding" part of the time. From Kenya Scouting songs in Swahili went on the air transmitted by 5Z4KSA in Paxtu, Nyeri. A Scout station in The Netherlands contacted Scouts in England operating from a factory where stockings were made for the Royal family; a quick deal was made: swap a few Dutch stockings for Royal ones...

Paul Bateman, G1ZOV and French NJO Luigi Malandrino, F6ICJ operate the special event station FF1SDF at the foot of the Eiffel Tower in Paris on the occasion of the World Scout Conference in July 1990.

Scouts in Zimbabwe operated Z27JAM and almost blew their radio tubes trying to contact HB9S at the World Scout Bureau in Geneva: they got through.

In Portugal the Scouts received permission to speak directly over the radio. Their press release reads: "of JOTA we can say that the World is embraced by youngsters proclaiming a world of peace, brotherhood and understanding".

The Geneva radio club HB9G in Petit Lancy loaned their facilities and equipment to the World Scout Bureau to operate HB9S during the JOTA for many years. Yves, HB9AOF and Peter, OZ1JZN are in action here in 1990.

The 34th JOTA 1991

In August 6K17WJ operates from the World Scout Jamboree held in South-Korea with varying success. Some 2000 contacts are made.

"Peace and Friendship through Communication" said the JOTA logo this year. Who would better understand the meaning of this than Scouts from the Eastern-European countries who now could take part in a direct contact with Scouts in the rest of the world. Scouts from the new organizations in Hungary and Czechoslovakia were on the air, as well as the many stations representing

Richard Middelkoop

emerging Scout organizations in Poland, Romania, Ukraine, Yugoslavia and the Baltic States. A unique opportunity to learn more about each others way of life.

Other countries were there on the airwaves for the first time or back after years of absence. Close to a 100 countries in total. The 34th JOTA saw more reports than before from participating countries: 43 in total. The JOTA letter game kept many of us busy during the weekend. On Sunday, we at HE7S listened in on a contact between a French and a British station who were swapping letters. Would the French Scouts trade an A and an M for a P and an S?

The 35th JOTA 1992

In May many National JOTA Organizers met in Denmark for the 3rd Radio-Scouting seminar. It was intended as a European seminar, but it attracted participants from as far away as Canada, Tanzania and Australia! Very useful were discussions we had with the new JOTA organizers of Scout Associations in Central- and Eastern European countries.

The Asia-Pacific Scout Conference was held in Jakarta in November and took an important decision regarding the Radio-Scouting programme. Conference resolution 27/92-iv reads: "International events such as World Scout Jamborees, COMDECA and Regional events may be linked with Scout Amateur Radio activities so that Scouts and Guides who are participating in these events may be able to spread the spirit and the message of such events internationally".

"Let's talk" said the JOTA logo this year. And so we did. At HB9S we noted especially more Scouts from Hungary and Czechoslovakia on the air, as well as from Poland, Romania, Ukraine and the Baltic States.

The World Federation of Great Towers invited Scouts to take part in the JOTA from the top of their Towers. This meant some extra organization work (where do I put my antennas? There are already so many of them here). It was a unique opportunity to install Scout stations on towers like the Eiffel Tower in Paris, The Empire State Building in New York and the CN Tower in Toronto, to name just a few. Scout displays and JOTA workshops were held at those stations and attracted many visitors.

In Japan one group

CQ Jamboree

organised English classes for their Scouts every Wednesday for some time. The Scouts were taught to explain the World Letter game to their foreign friends in English.....

Side activities in Norway included not only an axe competition and baking wafers, but also building a loo...... Turkey organized a post-JOTA meeting with a display of material from the countries that had been contacted. Embassies provided information and a translation of basic words into the respective languages. In Austria all radio amateurs were allowed to have the figure 35 in their call sign during the whole month of October to celebrate the 35th JOTA.

Scouts at the prestigious Omani JOTA station A47JOTA.

In Dartmouth, Canada the Naval Reserve demonstrated semaphore and Morse code for the Scouts.

One station in Czechoslovakia was manned by "Scouts", ages between 50 and 72. Hong Kong issued a Morse code training programme for a computer. Scouts in Lebanon shook the last bit of energy out of their car battery to operate their station.

The 36th JOTA 1993

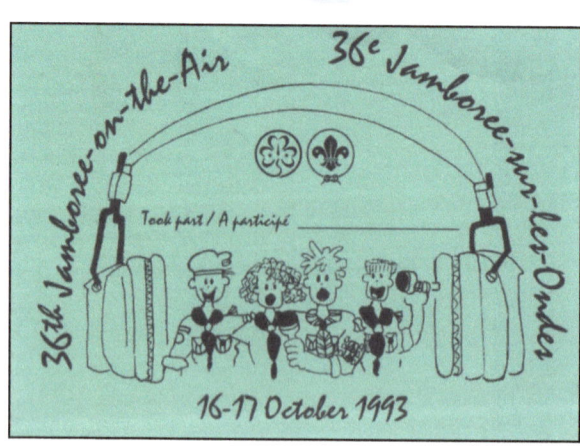

The radio propagation conditions co-operated well and the Scout frequencies were absolutely crowded.

Deaf Scouts used light signals to transmit and receive messages in Sierra Leone. A Mexican activity competition; one of the activities is to create 4 other activities. A Scout's investiture in the United Kingdom used a radio link to recite his promise. A Morse-code display set up in a church in Germany, attracting many visitors after the Mass. Automated reporting was introduced in The Netherlands with computer discs.

An FM broadcast station in Australia relayed JOTA contacts in its programme, with many listeners phoning in with reactions. Switching your transmitter with just 2 bare wires is possible when your Austrian Scouts forget to bring a CW key. Canadian Scouts broadcasted their JOTA QSO's during a wedding party through the speaker system of the nearby church......

The 37th JOTA 1994

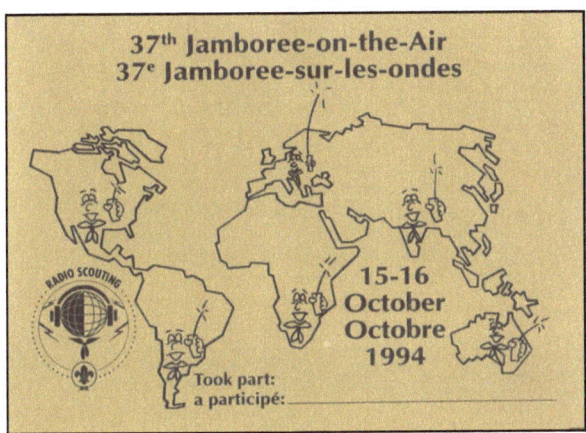

Of particular interest is the twinning activity organised by Mexico and Norway. To stimulate the international exchange, mutual activities were organised by the two countries with outstanding success. It is worth considering such an activity for other countries too. In fact, it is fully in line with the "Marakech Charter", concluded at a gathering of 118 Scout Associations in Morocco this year, which stated:" ......partnerships need to meet the young people's needs and aspirations..... and serve to enrich the youth programmes of the Scout Associations concerned..... and train them to acquire a good understanding of their own culture and that of their partners..... Modern means of communications offer undreamt-of possibilities to establish contacts and form links among people."

Radio conditions during the JOTA weekend were fabulous and HB9S kept running pile-ups all through the night. In Mauritius, Scouts held a sand-castle contest on the beach during JOTA. One JOTA station radio-contacted a taxi driver in Christchurch, New Zealand and his passenger joined in the contact.

Scouts in The Netherlands had to call the local fire brigade to rescue their antenna tower from falling over.

In Turkey, Scouts installed their JOTA station in a boxing ring. Cub Scouts in the US were wondering why radio did hurt so much, as their operator was explaining them

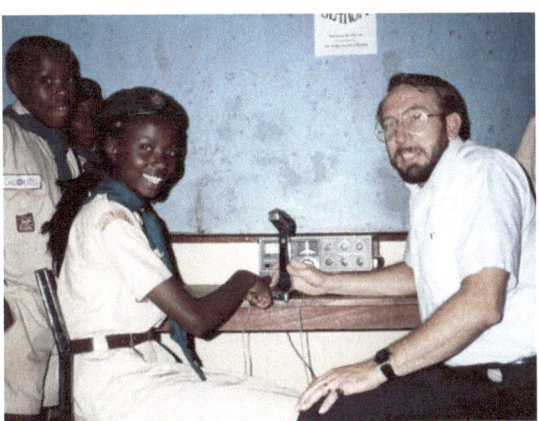

JOTA from a special place: 5Z4KSA at Paxtu Cottage, Nyeri, Kenya.

CQ Jamboree

about Megahurts. And in Poland a big bird kept landing on the antenna of a JOTA station and changed the polarity each time.

The 38th JOTA 1995

"The worst radio conditions ever......". Almost every report complained about the "radio weather" during the JOTA weekend. What happened? The ionosphere, a layer around the earth that reflects radio signals, was in bad shape. Like an old mirror that doesn't reflect the light too well. The 38th JOTA took place in the sunspot minimum.

At HB9S in Geneva we had a record time to sleep during the nights; all amateur radio bands produced just noise. Alternative techniques brought help: amateur radio satellites, digital terrestrial links and the internet.

Many Scouts organized electronic kit building sessions. A new phenomenon was the use of computer communications via Internet. The World JOTA Report had a separate section with the experiences of Scouts using this modern way of "talking" to each other.

During the summer many radio stations operated from large national or international summer camps. Some camps even maintained regular skeds to exchange information with each other. One of these camps was the 18th World Scout Jamboree in Dronten, The Netherlands.

The 39th JOTA 1996

The use of internet communications increased this year. Almost all Scout groups that used it, did so in combination with a radio station. This is consistent with the trend of using other techniques than just voice radio to communicate. For years packet-radio has been used for JOTA as well, using computers to type messages. Using internet is regarded as just another technique available for JOTA.

"¡¡ Hola todos, aqui 6E3ASM en Parque de la Chora, Mexico!!".

Richard Middelkoop

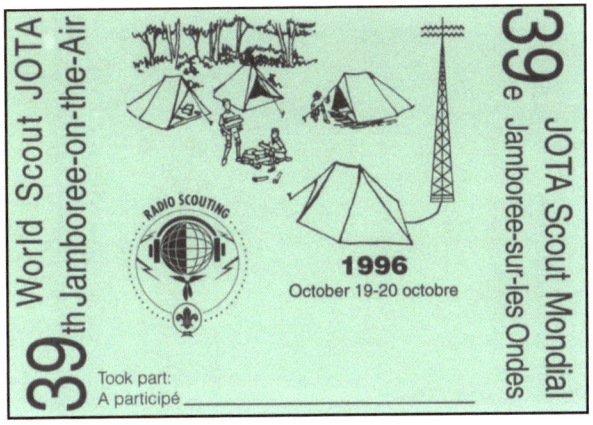

The participation increased notably in countries that saw another type of government come to power and now have well established Scout Associations who enjoy the free exchange of ideas via the airwaves with fellow Scouts.

A map co-ordinate game by radio in the UK proved very popular. Some stations prepared computerized presentations for visitors and left them running all weekend. SSTV and packet-radio were amongst the popular modes. The Keppel / Wiarton Regional Airport in Canada hosted the JOTA station of the 1st Wiarton Scouts, in a vacated flight services office. Scouts in Australia used a 3-way ATV link, including a commercial satellite, to participate in a "Scouts Own" on the Sunday morning. Their JOTA opening was transmitted over a linked network of shortwave- and VHF stations. The national JOTA station in Austria was set up in the ruins of a medieval castle....under canvas.

One of the "new" JOTA stations: OK5SCT in Prague, Czechoslovakia with operator Jirka and his Scouts.

The Habo Scout group in Sweden connected a computer to their radio and to internet, so everyone could see at which frequency they were transmitting. What an easy way to find a station on the airwaves. A popular electronic kit to assemble during JOTA comes from China: Scouts in Tapei produced a music playing, flashing radio-scouting badge.

Shortly before the World Scout Conference in Oslo, Norway, I was invited to go there. I took a while before I became aware why this was the case. A letter from Geneva arrived, informing me that the World Scout Committee had decided to present me the Bronze Wolf award, WOSM's only recognition for service to the Movement. I learned lateron that my XYL had been in the plot much earlier already.... Driving into Oslo with my family, I checked in by radio on a local repeater, only to discover that many Norwegian radio friends had come to Oslo as well; and I thought I kept it a secret...; we all had a party at the house of Nick Holter, LA5CH after the ceremony.

CQ Jamboree

The new era of electronic communication

By the end of the nineties, the world had drastically changed: internet had arrived. JOTA reports from National Scout Associations began to arrive via email. No more thick and heavy packages for the mailman in my home town. It also meant less stamps from various parts in the world, sadly enough for my relatives who are enthusiastic stamp collectors.

But the reports were considerably faster in arriving and I could start editing them in an electronic way. Much more flexibility in lay-outing the World JOTA Report. I could also send the camera-ready copy to Geneva, first on computer disks. That did present one problem as the Bureau in Geneva worked with Macintosh computers and I am using PC's. I had to use a conversion programme to read the floppy disks. With the arrival of email this problem was solved of course.

The fast internet development even resulted in another annual world-wide Scout meeting, the Jamboree On The Internet, JOTI. At first regarded by many radio amateurs as an unwanted competitor. The World Scout Committee decided, however, to have the JOTI as a separate event, but on the same weekend as JOTA. This turned out to be a wise move; the two events could still benefit from each other's techniques, but Scouts had a choice to take part in one or the other or even both. The Committee decision meant that I should concentrate on the amateur radio matters only and no longer be involved in the internet developments like I had been for the previous 3 years leading up to the JOTI creation. From now on, the JOTI should have its own organizer, information leaflets and annual report. It turned out that it took several years before this became a reality and its organization still leaned heavily on the JOTA structure.

My JOTA point of contact at the Bureau passed over to Mark Clayton, the director of public relations and communications. Mark was very supportive of the event and a regular guest at the Radio-Scouting seminars held in Europe periodically.

The 40th JOTA 1997

The 40th jubilee JOTA did not go unnoticed: several specialities were set up.

Many groups soldered the one-wire telephone set that was published in the first JOTA info circular.

A propagation prediction for the JOTA was made by the Danish Meteorological Institute and broadcasted on national TV during the weather forecast following the main news.

The radio team in the United Kingdom designed a Q-code domino game. Scouts in Australia used a balloon to attach their antenna to. A handicapped Portuguese radio amateur made contacts in Braille.

Richard Middelkoop

Scouts in Switzerland operated from a giant tree cabin at 20 m high. In The Netherlands, a group of rover Scouts were dropped many miles away from home. Walking back they visited every JOTA station and reported their progress by radio. The Scout group in Aschbach, Austria ran a post office and used a jubilee JOTA rubber stamp to mark the letters.

The World Scout Bureau moved its own amateur radio station to the very birthplace of the JOTA, in Reading, UK., being the guest of the 79th Reading Scouts. It was set up at the very same place where 40 years ago the 1st JOTA was held. The station GB/HB9S was operated by the JOTA founder Les Mitchell G3BHK, former World JOTA Organizer Len Jarrett VE3MYF who came over from Canada, and Yves HB9AOF, Richard PA3BAR, Jeff G3SDG, Alan G3WNS, John G4KGT, Geoff G4UEL, Ben G7WHO, and Barbara G8AKU.

Yves Margot HB9AOF, Richard Middelkoop PA3BAR and Len Jarrett VE3MYF (left to right) at the controls of GB/HB9S for the 40th JOTA in Reading, UK.

The station crew installed antennas that were similar to the ones used 40 years ago: two G5RV's and a dipole; just the radio equipment was modern.

Of particular interest was the contact with G3IKA, Mr. Arthur Hutchence. Forty years ago Arthur was the schoolmaster in Reading and had personally helped to set up the first JOTA station together with Les Mitchell. You can imagine the lively QSO we had with him, with Les at the microphone on our side.

Geoff overheard a conversation of an American Scout station with another UK JOTA station. The Americans commented what a wonderful idea the JOTA was and asked who dreamed up the idea. Obviously the station he was in contact with could not provide the answer to this query. Geoff called in and told him that he could not only tell him who was involved but he could also easily arrange for this person to speak to them. Les did so a few minutes later....

CQ Jamboree

The 4th European Radio Scouting seminar met in Jambville, near Paris, France in May with 34 participants from 17 different countries. They discussed JOTA and Radio-Scouting programmes, in particular the use of internet and a common European licence to allow Scouts to speak over the airwaves.

The 41st JOTA 1998

A change was announced of one of the traditional world Scout frequencies, the one on the 10 m band. With radio conditions improving we got many suggestions to change it into a more active part of the band.

A very determined radio amateur in Switzerland could not be stopped from participating in the JOTA. He was in hospital, but the Scouts put his station in a minibus in the hospital parking lot.

Scouts in Canada and The Netherlands ran a fox hunt with the help of a GPS receiver.

The Ministry of Telecommunications in China conducted official amateur radio exams during the JOTA weekend, especially for the Scouts, at novice level.

A combined JOTA - JOTI handbook was published in Spanish in Guatemala. Silk-printed T-shirts with a JOTA logo were available in Hong Kong. The WAGGGS centre Our Chalet in Switzerland was also on the air.

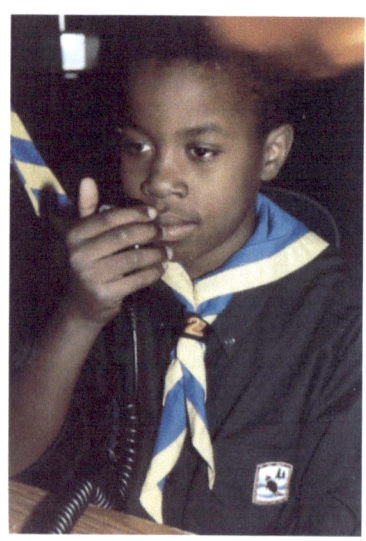

"Ici Marc de Quebec au Canada qui t'appèlle...."

The 42nd JOTA 1999

A combined radio and internet activity was the John Bont game. Scouts needed a radio station as well as internet access to solve this puzzle game. Not that many Scouts were able to find the correct solution.

Richard Middelkoop

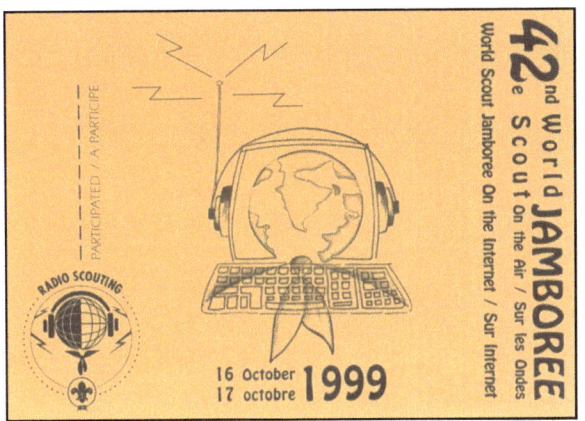

The design competition for electronic kit building was not a popular thing as we received just 1 official entry (UK). It did not fulfil all the requirements so the jury decided to give it a special mention but not to award any prices this time. Maybe the competition did not get a lot of national publicity or designing these kits is just a difficult job.

Quite a number of countries, however, mentioned the kit building activities for their Scouts, so one may conclude that the actual kit-building activity as such is popular among Scouts.

The 43rd JOTA 2000

Scouts in Dehsadun, India having fun in the JOTA from their school building.

36 participants representing 22 different Scout Associations met in Rome in May for the 5th European Radio Scouting and Internet Seminar. They discussed the future use of new technology for the JOTA.

From the reports it is apparent that most Scout groups used internet in combination with amateur radio stations. One combined activity was the Cartoon Network game. Scouts needed a radio station or internet access to take part in this game. The target was to find 5 different JOTA drawings and to design two others yourself, in order to make a complete cartoon story out of it.

A special antenna was designed by Scouts in Germany for the JOTA and is named *"Scout roof"*.

Chile organised a reunion at the National station for former Scouts and operators.

CQ Jamboree

The whole town made a community party out of the JOTA weekend.

A photo contest for the best JOTA picture was held in Denmark. Another activity was a kit-building project to create awareness for landmine problems. Scouts in Namibia cooked JOTA meals in a hay box.

In the USA, Scouts could see their own voices going on the air, by hooking up an oscilloscope to the microphone.

The World Scout Bureau operated with the special call sign HB2S, to celebrate the new millennium. To me this was a memorable JOTA, as for the first time I spoke over short-wave amateur radio with my own son and daughter who were first-time JOTA participants now at their Scout group Kiliaen van Rensselaer I in Nijkerk, The Netherlands.

*The HB2S team, from the top left to right:
Mich LX1KQ, Yves HB9AOF
Philippe LX2AJ, Lisbeth OZ1JRD
Richard PA3BAR, Frank M0AEU*

The 44th JOTA 2001

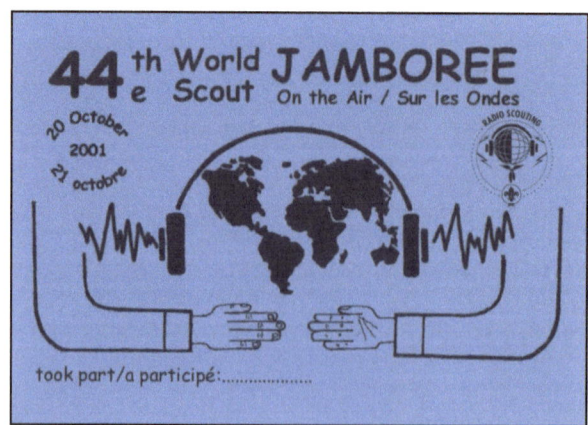

A JOTA report that landed in the mailbox from outer space. The 44th JOTA will go into history as the one where a voice came out of a Space station calling "CQ Jamboree". The commander of the International Space Station, himself a former Scout, took part in the JOTA event with NA1SS, while he was in orbit at 310 km above us. He gave JOTA a new dimension.

The 44th Jamboree On The Air was held in the turbulent aftermath of the tragic events in the USA. What influence it had is unclear, but we did see a significant drop in total participants world wide. The Jamboree on the Internet organizers also

Richard Middelkoop

reported a drop in activity with about half the previous year's visitors to the World Scouting website.

On the positive site, the JOTA weekend was blessed with excellent radio conditions. HF bands stayed open most of the night, depriving many operators from some hours of sleep. Since who wants to go to bed when there are still Scout stations you can contact? Several countries reported solid, long-distance contacts. In some cases high quality colour pictures were exchanged by radio too.

The International Space Station ISS participating in the 44th JOTA.

The 45th JOTA 2002

"Share our world, share our airwaves", could have been the JOTA variation to the World Scout Jamboree theme. Once you think you have seen it all, new ideas and possibilities enter the playing field. JOTA is no different to that. The 45th JOTA had things like Echolink and J-code to share our airwaves. Contacts with the International Space Station, initiated last year, were there again. And lots of "normal" radio contacts. With relatively good radio propagation throughout the weekend, many high-quality contacts were possible, even those over large distances.

e-QSO and Echolink are new technologies that seem to have found their way to JOTA. What is it? Basically a technique to transport radio signals to another place via the internet and retransmit them at the destination. In the case of Echolink, one can make a direct contact with a computer to this virtual radio channel and participate in the communication. In fact, a large open network is the result, which has participants connected via radio and

Brazil: a JOTA camp site with a view......

CQ Jamboree

others via the internet directly. Isn't that wonderful? JOTA and JOTI come together as one big Scout network. This would open up a whole new gamma of possibilities for the Scouts participating in JOTA and JOTI. Surely to be continued with new experiments in the coming years.

The J-code was another experiment this year. A simple code has been designed by Dave Gemmell of South Africa. It should help to overcome the ever-present language barrier during radio or internet contacts by offering simple codes for an elementary conversation. Much like the Q-code does for radio amateurs. The J-code has been translated into many different languages. Reports show that some Scout groups used it enthusiastically, whilst others thought it was rather difficult. In any case, it is not easy to get used to it. But the Scouts who did use it commented: "better a difficult communication than no communication". I can imagine the Morse code had a similar start…….

The 46th JOTA 2003

By exception, the World Scout Bureau operated with two stations: HB9S in Geneva and DA0WSB at the international Scout centre IPT in Kalkar, Germany. The intent was to run some tests between them with new communication techniques.

Several countries that broadcasted an official JOTA opening ceremony used the internet in parallel to the short-wave radio. This gave a much wider coverage.

The J-code was again an experiment this year.

Another remarkable experiment was done by Scouts in Argentina, who used translation software on a web site to quickly translate a conversation into their own language. It did slow down the contact a bit, but was fun and interesting to do.

And speaking of experiments, how's this one? Scouts in Istanbul participated in a marathon run. While doing so, they reported their progress to Scouts in other countries, using portable radios and the Echolink system.

In June, 35 National JOTA - JOTI Organizers and team members from 14 different countries convened in Rieneck, Germany for the 6th European Radio Scouting and Internet Seminar. Many aspects of JOTA and JOTI were discussed. On the agenda were workshops that dealt in particular with publicity, educational methods, international cooperation in organizing and internet use.

Richard Middelkoop

Amateur Radio and beyond

By now, JOTA had expanded beyond the traditional use of short-wave radio. The amateur-radio community had introduced the first systems that could link radio transmitters and receivers via the internet. In fact, one could operate an amateur radio transmitter in another country remotely, via an internet link. Of course, JOTA stations were amongst the first to experiment with it. After extensive consultation with the system owners, I choose the Echolink system as the most suited for JOTA. At the time, child safety on the internet was a growing concern (and still is). Echolink provides for additional safety, since only registered radio amateurs could use it and licences are checked before access to the system is granted.

Echolink provided for long-distance contacts with Scout stations, even if HF radio propagation was not there. A great new opportunity arose, in particular for countries like Australia. All of a sudden DX Scout contacts were possible and in good quality too. From a camp site, out in the middle of nowhere, Scouts could still access the Echolink system with a small radio linked to a local repeater. Speak to the world with a handheld radio from your tent! Magnificent.

It was not without controversy, however. Many radio amateurs argued that the use of an internet section in between the radio link was "cheating". Others however, underlined that it was better to offer a Scout the possibility to speak with other Scouts than just have him listen to the eternal noise fields at times without radio propagation. After all, JOTA was meant to make contacts possible.

The Scouts of China at their amateur radio station in Taipei.

As an experiment, I created a World Scout Net, one that convenes once each month, linked together via a combination of short-wave radio and Echolink. For the first time, a conference was possible with participants from all corners of the world at the same time. I found a good friend from the 1983 World Scout Jamboree, Al Davidson, VE6DE, and his Scout group in Alberta, Canada, prepared to host the Echolink conference node on a server at their premises. To find a convenient time for all was not easy; in the end we agreed on midnight in Europe, which is mid-afternoon in the America's and early morning in the Far-East.

The Radio-Scouting web site becomes increasingly important to distribute JOTA information to all Scout Associations. For those with internet access, the web offers a fast and easy source of information. The JOTA circulars, printed on paper, are maintained, however, to ensure that information reached those less fortunate and still enable them to take part in the event.

CQ Jamboree

The 47th JOTA 2004

In Australia and the UK a new foundation radio licence offered many Scouts a chance to obtain their own radio permit. Many more young Scout radio operators took part in the JOTA event.

In Canada, roughly 500 km south of the Arctic Circle, members of the 1st Porter Creek Scouts from Whitehorse, Yukon Territory, camped out in -10°C. Whilst at the same time in the Czech Republic, girl Guides baked delicious JOTA pancakes. In Geneva, the new Secretary General Eduardo Missoni had his first radio contact. Dutch Scouts competed with each other with a weather-station contest. In Hungary, JOTA is a family business as licensed grandparents put their Scout-grand-children on the air. And the J-code was there again to break the language barrier.

During JOTA in Turkey, a 15-year-old Girl Guide with her own radio station saved 10 people from a fire in a 200 m deep mine. JOTA is not only a fun experience; it also gives Scouts the ability to "be prepared", said the National JOTA Organizer.

Right after the JOTA, during Christmas 2004, a Tsunami wave struck Asia and created a disaster. Scout radio-amateurs and Scouts trained in JOTA were involved in running emergency communications for disaster relief operations. Scouts of the E20AJ team of the World Scout Jamboree held in 2003 in Thailand, were amongst those who responded. Together with members of RAST (Radio Amateur Society of Thailand) they operated 2m and 40m from Dec 27th onwards, linked to Phuket and southern Thailand and forwarded information via internet and Echolink, as well as over VHF frequencies in Bangkok.

The 48th JOTA 2005

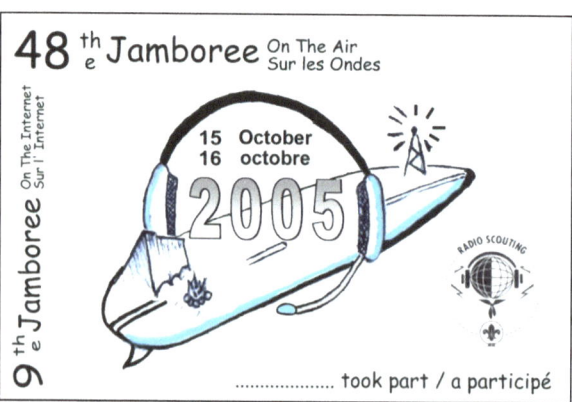

Echolink, a system that connects amateur-radio stations and internet users together, was used more extensively this year. It overcomes long-distance radio propagation difficulties by routing the radio signal partly over the internet and allows contact with Scouts in remote locations, where there is no

Richard Middelkoop

internet, by using a radio link. Great for JOTA and very promising for special activities during the Centenary in 2007!

In Argentina, the cook at the station of the Foxes of the San Javier group, was speaking by radio (and not watching his cooking!) so the stew burned. The Argentine Mail Service made a postal seal, which was applied to the mail of the most austral city of the world, "Ushuaia".

Scouts in Bangladesh organized the national JOTA camp on the hill top of Shitakunda; everything had to carried from 800 meters down. Power from solar panels and dry food was supplied.

In Belize the Scouts collected how to say "be prepared" in many different languages.

Scout group 920 in Hungary had HA5FQ on the air, operated by a 10-year old Guide!

A yearly Swiss challenge is to have the highest station above sea level. This year a station at the top on Monte Ceneri, 2978m asl, won.

Dutch Scouts need high towers to get their JOTA antenna above sea level....

Changes at the Bureau....

At the end of 2005, the Secretary General announced some drastic changes in the staff of the World Scout Bureau. Various departments were re-organized and staff and directors changed positions or left the Bureau. The office space was allocated differently and the permanent shack of HB9S in the office disappeared. The antennas on the roof remained, but the cables into the building were now rendered useless. The JOTA point of contact was transferred to Richard Amalvy, the new communications director. As it turned out, Richard's focus was on the public image of JOTA. Colourful participation cards started to appear, drawn by a professional designer and were no longer based on a suggestion from a JOTA youth participant. The lay-out of the World JOTA Report was also effected by his approach. The increased quality of the printed material unfortunately also had a downside: it took far longer to produce, giving me several headaches in trying to get it to the Scout Associations in time for JOTA.

The 49th JOTA 2006

The 7th European Radio-Scouting and Internet Seminar came together in Oslo in June. 42 participants from 21 different countries (even 1 from New Zealand) discussed the approach towards the interference of the Worked All Germany (WAG) contest, played with the Dutch Scout laser game, visited a war museum with clandestine radio's and looked at plans for the 2007 activities.

CQ Jamboree

For the JOTA, Scouts at Heidenreichstein in Austria attached their antenna to a 25m high observation tower.

In Bangladesh, Scouts had set up their JOTA station at the beach of the Bay of Bengal and held an ARDF tournament.

Scouts in Belize struggled with the language, trying to explain to their Portuguese brothers how to send a QSL card. White Pine Council in Canada organized a large JOTA camp. The "highlight" was a police helicopter fly-by, over the camp site, shining its searchlight on the Scouts.

The AO 51 amateur radio satellite was frequently used during JOTA, particularly in India and Sudan.

The Scouts in Dublin, Ireland operated from the Martello tower, a former Marconi test site, while Scouts in Larch Hill, Mount Melleray and Clontarf had a one-hour contact with the Karratha Scout group in NW Australia.

In Malta, a Scout leader forgot to eat his birthday pizza, because he was so busy with the radio contacts.

The pioneered antenna tower of one group in The Netherlands was higher than the local church tower......

In Oman, the Scouts had a very creative JOTA and composed the JOTA song and a JOTA movie.

One special QSO in Portugal, with Scouts in Brazil; it started via radio, then using Echolink, IRC and Skype with a webcam.

In Irene, South-Africa, the radio station was set up in the "store room", built in the old water reservoir of the town. In Sudan, Scouts operated ST2KSS from the Crocodile Island of the Sea Scouts camp, powered by solar cells.

How do you get your antenna wires high up in the trees? Well ask the Scouts in the US: they used a tennis ball launcher to do the job. Also they discovered that cooking grills are excellent as heaters.

Cub Scouts in Hong Kong having fun in the 49th JOTA.

Richard Middelkoop

The 50th JOTA 2007

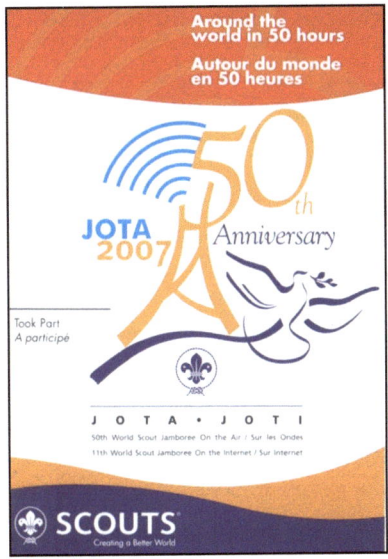

JOTA started early this year, at 22:00 h local time on the Friday. Two hours earlier than normal, and this was just what we needed to have 50 hours for the Jubilee 50th JOTA: "Around the world in 50 hours".

After long negotiations with the German Amateur Radio Club DARC, led by former German NJO's Klaus Sperling and Günter Erdmann and supported by the IARU, an agreement was reached to stop interference between the JOTA and the Worked All Germany contest (WAG). This contest, East-German by origin, is the only contest in the JOTA weekend, contrary to earlier agreements. As of this year, the WAG maintained large contest-free sections on the Amateur Bands. The Scout frequencies were slightly shifted as well so in the end the WAG kept all Scout frequencies in the clear. Well done!

Well-known radio-scouter Frank Heritage introduced the prestigious Centenary of Scouting Radio Award, available in 5 levels, aimed at making Scout radio contacts. This really boosted the activity of Radio-Scouting stations during the whole of 2007 and especially during JOTA.

The World Scout Bureau operated HB50S from the Satigny Scout centre with excellent results: we never before contacted so many Scout stations world-wide. If it weren't the very modest propagation conditions, than it was certainly due to the enthusiasm of the crew and Günter's special antenna system with switched four-square full-sized verticals on 40 m.

The 22nd Asia-Pacific Regional Conference convened in Tokyo over the JOTA weekend and had a first in opening the 50th JOTA. World Scout Committee chairman Herman Hui and Secretary General Eduardo Missoni spoke over radio 8J1S from the Conference room to the world. A team from the Scout amateur radio club of

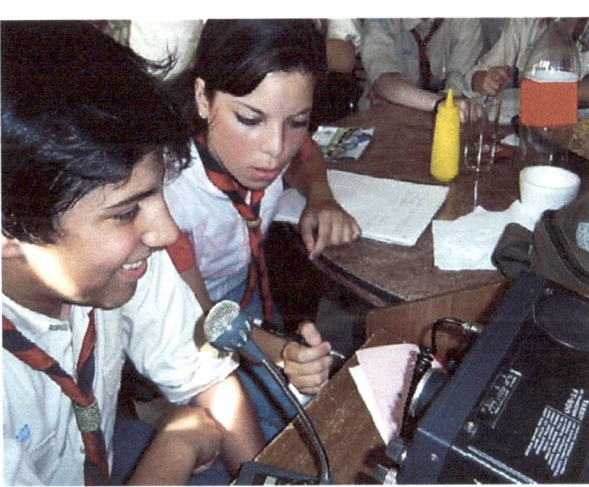

Scouts of the Equipo de Comunicaciones Z22 in Córdoba, Argentina discussing plans for new Scout activities.

CQ Jamboree

the Japanese Headquarters, led by Tat Mochiki, JH1FEL, guided the radio traffic.

In Norway, a special call sign was obtained for the 50th JOTA, the LC prefix where L is 50 for the 50th JOTA and C is 100 for 100 years of Scouting.

Scouts in the Netherlands Antilles could participate in numerous communication games and activities and also in a yell competition and an outrageous cooking contest. Scouts in two JOTA camps in Bangladesh sang 50 songs together.

One young Scout in South Africa travelled on foot for over 35 km to the special JOTA camp in Mafikeng. Scouts in Turkey wrote 50 letters to themselves for 2057. These will be delivered to them at the 100th JOTA.

An earthquake in the city of Pisco in Peru two months before JOTA, swung Scout radio amateurs into action for emergency communications. This has motivated many Scouts to take an interest in radio.

In Oman, Scout contacted other Scouts in a staggering 111 different countries. Mainly due to having one separate Echolink station per continent installed at the Scout HQ station.

Scouts in the Czech Republic commented: the best idea for the next JOTA? To have some radio propagation!!

The 51st JOTA 2008

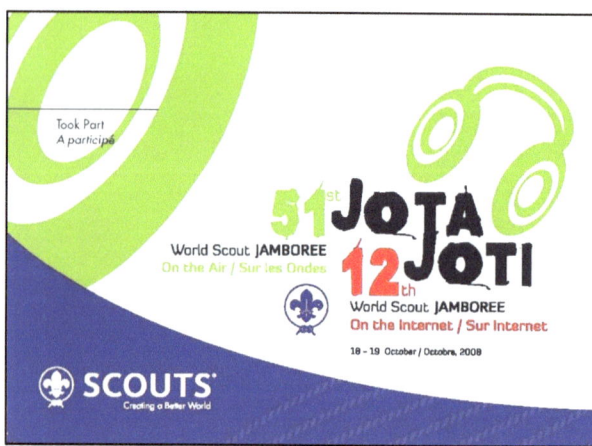

For the first time, we also used the input of the international web logs to compile the World JOTA Report, for those countries of which we did not receive a national report. The World JOTA Report no longer appeared in printed form. With current technology, the report can be presented on the internet in full colour and within hours of being finished. The WAG contest continued to voluntarily maintain large contest-free sections. A complete translation into Chinese of the JOTA circulars and other information was nicely made into a JOTA Seminar Handbook in Taiwan.

Venture Scouts from the capital in Estonia were very motivated to come to ES5JOTA, which was 120 km away. They arrived first in Jõgeva by train. They decided to hike the remaining 13 km to the station on foot, across a forest and they had to pass over a river.

Cub Scouts are very keen on walky-talkies; great fun.

Richard Middelkoop

Alternative power sources were explored by Genova Scouts in Italy. They got electricity from tin cans, filled with bleach.

PA6BUS/J in The Netherlands travelled in an converted public transport bus, and the national station PA6JAM/J was maritime mobile on a retired freight vessel. Both travelled hundreds of kilometers and could be followed via APRS and live video.

In South-Africa, one of the displays in the "wireless room" were two old field telephones which had to be connected together with suitable wire….. (in the "wireless room"?).

Most of the JOTA stations in Turkey participated in the "Stand up" event to support the UN Millennium Development Goal on the elimination of poverty.

The art of building Scout antenna towers for JOTA

The 52nd JOTA 2009

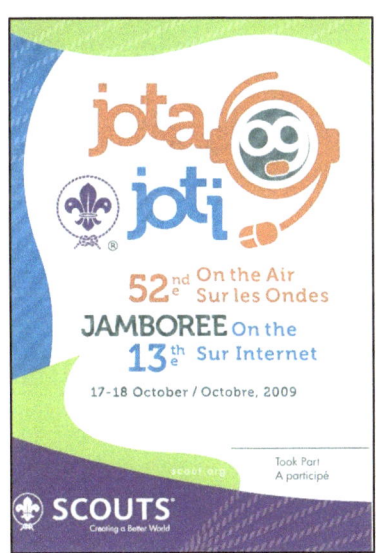

The JOTA had a climate theme: the C3 challenge. It was intended to create awareness of the upcoming climate conference in Copenhagen.

The World Scout Bureau had invited several Scout groups from the Geneva area to enjoy the event with us at HB9S. Unlike other years, we had a very lively "background QRM" this time.

A hydroelectric power generator was constructed in Estonia, made from car- and bicycle parts to power the radio station. The generator was powered by a local unused water dyke.

A most interesting contact between the Secretary General of WOSM and the National Chief Scout to talk about the developments of Scouting in Guinea Bissau.

The programme in Iceland began with a midnight swim with 69 people in a Jacuzzi.

An earthquake struck the town of l'Aquila in Italy. Many people still lived in tents!

CQ Jamboree

A JOTA station was set up among these tents. It offered a Scout event to those Scouts and Guides struck by the earthquake.

A discussion on climate change was held in Madagascar via radio. In parallel, a Guide was present in Copenhagen, bringing thousands of signatures of Scouts willing to engage in the challenge.

Radio operations in New Zealand had to come to a halt several times, due to the noise level of the rain on the roof!

Earlier in the year, European National JOTA Organizers and their team members met at Ulfjotsvatn in Iceland for the 8th tri-annual Radio-Scouting seminar.

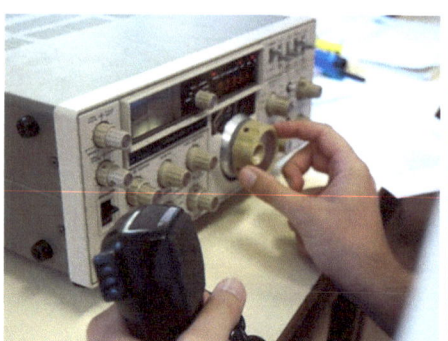

"…….we just turned our antenna, so we can hear you better….."

The 53rd JOTA 2010

Jampuz, a JOTA-JOTI bingo game, was introduced this year. Quite popular amongst those having a go at it.

Specially for Scout stations, a DX cluster was put on line by the amateur radio club in Zoetermeer, The Netherlands.

The report mentioned that 80% of the JOTA radio operators in Brazil are Scouts themselves.

A special station OL120ORT was set up for the 120th anniversary of the Czech radio pioneer Karel Ort, at the same place where his experimental short wave station was built back in 1908.

A leader in French Polynesia, complained of not being able to speak with one of her contacts; it turned out, she had forgotten to connect the microphone…..

Scouts in Hungary disassembled electronic devices to see "what is inside."

Richard Middelkoop

Connecting Scouts......

Scouts in Malta took turns through the radio using the phonetic alphabet. One of the Scouts repeated a call sign which contained a YD in it. This Scout's anxiety rose so much that when he reached the YD part, he said Yankee Doodle.....after which all the room starting laughing.

A girl scout from the 972 group in Midões Portugal, won the Radio-Scouting merit badge, having received a Morse Code transmission at 20 words per minute; her group was one of those that never joined JOTA before.

National Coordinator Dave Gemmel writes: "I hope the rest of the Scouting World has "forgiven" South-Africa for "inventing" the Morse code game by Vuvuzela!!"

Scouts practising Morse code on the Vuvuzela, quite a hype in 2010!

The 54th JOTA 2011

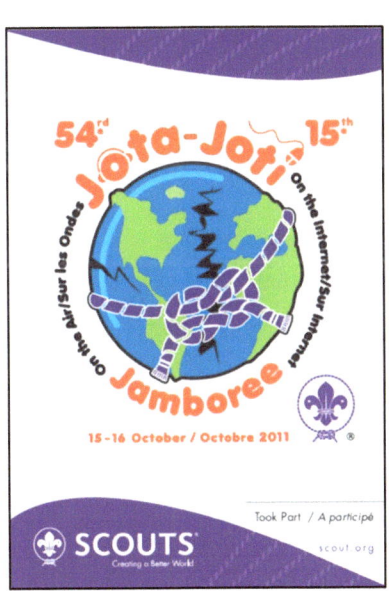

A survey amongst NJO's, about interference of the WAG contest with the new contest-free zones showed only a small number of incidents.

The theme activity was about natural disaster relief work and the Scoutonia emergency exercise; it involved IARU and Shelterbox officials, both at world and local levels.

Scouts from Chios in Greece contacted Curacao! The area is so far away, they did

JOTA: great fun!

Girl Scouts at GB2GP, Gilwell Park, UK

not know it existed and searched the world map to find it.

Malaysia held a radio communication simulation, named 'SEEN' (Scouts Emergency Exercise Nationwide).

The Minister of Traffic, Transport and Urban Planning in the Netherlands Antilles visited the JOTA station.

In The Netherlands, 8 Groups succeeded in communicating to each other via the moon; using EME with a 25m radio telescope dish that was connected to the internet.

A leader in South-Africa demonstrated sending his call sign using Morse on a vuvuzela! A young Scout fell off his chair, whether from fright or laughter I wasn't told.

Group 235 in Portugal used a petrol generator and a dipole for messages for the Scoutonia exercise. One activity was search and rescue with trained dogs in an earthquake simulated scene.

In Turkey, JOTA began with messages titled "THIS IS AN EXERCISE". A week later Scouts continued with sad messages beginning with "THIS IS NOT AN EXERCISE": a devastating earthquake in the South-East of Turkey hit a town. Thanks to JOTA, Scouts were prepared.

An "earthquake" occurred in Suffolk, UK. It brought down the TA33jnr beam. The 'International Rescue Team' pondered the damage to the beam. Fortunately, the Scouts were able to repair the damage before the camp warden saw it.

Some JOTA antennas are quite modest…..

One station in the USA made a contact with NA1SS on the International Space Station using a Yagi made out of barbed wire.

The 55th JOTA 2012

In May, 47 National JOTA and JOTI Organizers met in Porto, Portugal for the 9th ERSIS. Jim Parnell, the NJC of New Zealand, came over and presented a glimpse of history with audio visuals of the first radio-scouting conference in 1975. In July I was fortunate to also visit the *"Vis Tes Rêves"* National Jamboree in Jambville,

France. The Radio-Scouting stand was very popular; 600 participants took part in several radio activities. On the HAM Radio fair in Friedrichshafen, Germany, Scouts were represented with a booth.

A first: the World JOTA Report had bar codes included with web links to audio- and video materials. And Ham Radio Deluxe software plotted a contact map and displayed it live on the internet, together with the actual operating frequency.

A campaign launched in Brazil named "one radio amateur in each Scout group". Stations in Canada combined outdoor camping with emergency preparedness; amateur radio is essential in the event of disasters.

My fist QSO....Scouts of China

A group of Scouts in Estonia had an excursion to the satellite ESTCube project. ES5JOTA was based there. Dutch astronaut Andre Kuipers opened the JOTA in The Netherlands.

A JOTA station was set up in Al Balid City, Oman, the ancient port on the Arabian Sea whose history dates back to before 2000 BC.

Scouts in South-Africa did not had electricity; so they used a very long extension lead from a house across the road (with all the traffic driving across it all day!!)

Max Stiles, in the USA wrote: "I do not think I can precisely express in words the wonderful experience for all our Scouts. They had in 30 hours, combined lessons that will last a lifetime".

Night time at a Dutch JOTA campsite.

CQ Jamboree

The 56th JOTA 2013

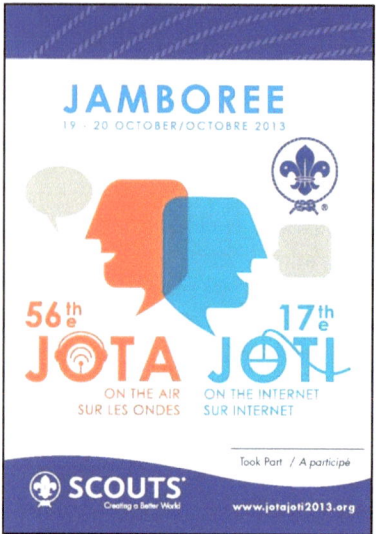

The World Scout Committee decided in 2013, that JOTA and JOTI should be one integrated event, as opposed to two separate ones on the same weekend, a change of their decision in 1997 at the initiation of JOTI. This was triggered by growing concerns of the then JOTI team about their ability to upscale their systems and keep them going. The JOTI activity was transferred to the WOSM web.

Argentina organized "the challenge of Akela", where Cubs had to find data on the other pack, using a chat room. Scouts in France commented: "We spent the night in an amateur station that looked like a space shuttle. There were bizarre devices all around us".

The 13-year-old girl Seraina Diekmann in Namibia had her first two QSO´s a bit shaky... but after the 3rd one they could not get her away from the radio. And after about 1.5 hours she took over the station completely.

Bright Morse code and flag-code transmissions were organized in collaboration with the Portuguese Navy; signals were transmitted from a land station to a corvette based near the port of Ponta Del-gada.

Young operators in action.

USA introduced the amateur radio operator strip for uniform wear by all licensed Scout amateur radio operators.

Farewell to HB9S: the World Scout Bureau operated HB9S from the Satigny Scout centre, for the very last time, as the Bureau was moving to Kuala Lumpur in the course of 2014. For this occasion, station manager Yves Margot and myself invited all the

Wireless radio....usually requiring a lot of wires locally......

operators who had ever helped to run HB9S from Geneva in the past. We managed to get a good size group together for our "reunion operation" and the HB9S farewell party. Together we managed to make the largest number of Scout contacts ever in HB9S' 43-years JOTA history.

Richard Middelkoop

Merge and Move

Following the World Scout Committee's decision to integrate JOTA and JOTI, John Lawlor, the World Scout Bureau World Events director at the time, asked me during the JOTA of 2013 in Satigny if I would be willing to lead both JOTA and JOTI and merge them into one event. And to recruit a new organization team for it. Shortly before, the JOTI team had been disbanded. I had to give the matter a few thoughts as some commotion and emotion had erupted amongst those involved when the former JOTI team left the scene. In the end, I agreed and started to work on the new organization.

Early 2014, John and myself launched a call for volunteers to apply. A careful selection process followed, including on-line interviews via Skype. Finally, 5 volunteers were pre-selected and presented to the World Scout Committee. The Commitee appointed the volunteers and I got the job of coordinating both JOTA and JOTI, leading the team and further integrating the two streams into one event.

The merger as such appeared not to be a "walk in the park". We approached some members of the former JOTI team to take a role in the new organization, in particular for the existing features on the web site. This, however, was not met with enthusiasm. Earlier, the World Scout Bureau staff decided that for 2013 the JOTI features would be transferred to the WOSM *scout.org* web site. This integration appeared far from easy as the content management system on *scout.org* offered less possibilities than the event needed. Some of the well-known features were kept, others were not and new possibilities were added. Somehow we managed to get the basics running in time for the 2013 JOTA-JOTI.

The new team, now called "World JOTA-JOTI Team" or WJJT for short, met in March 2014 in Geneva, alongside with the World Scout Committee meeting. We spent quite some time on getting to know each other better, understanding the items each team member wanted a role in, and dividing the work items that needed to be addressed. Two deputy World Organizers were nominated, Hannu Rättö, OH7GIG, with a JOTA background and Ali al-Marmari for JOTI. Philip Bird would look after games and event promotion, whilst Jim Wilson, K5ND, took care of social media and event communications. With direct support from the World Scout Bureau in Geneva offered by John Lawlor, World Events Director. The World Scout Committee nominated Mari Nakano as the Committee's liaison person for the WJJT. I was allowed a short presentation of the team and our new plans before the entire World Scout Committee. Luckily, these were met with enthusiasm and we were supported to continue along the way I had presented.The Team decided on a separate event web site that offered more flexibility; www.world-jotajoti.info was launched with close links to the main WOSM web site www.scout.org. Several on-line meetings followed, in preparation of the 2014 event.

Amidst this change in JOTA-JOTI organization, came another challenge: the move of the World Scout Bureau from Geneva to Kuala Lumpur. Which had been decided a few years earlier after a thorough investigation for a suitable place by the World Scout Committee. The move also brought along a large number of staff changes. Which meant a fresh start in "KL" as we referred to the new Bureau location. Team meetings would henceforth be held in Kuala Lumpur and no longer in Geneva. To me personally, this meant a much longer flight and a larger bite into the holiday budget that I had for absence from my regular work (did I mention I am a volunteer too?).

CQ Jamboree

9M4WSB appears…..

The move to Malaysia also implicated we needed to move the WSB permanent amateur radio station. Luckily, I found the National JOTA Organizer Zakran Abdul Manan in Malaysia willing to help and apply for a Malaysian station license. The much-appreciated support we received from MARTS, the Malaysian amateur radio transmitters society, was vital in the process as well. After some deliberation and consulting the authorities, the World Scout Bureau was kindly granted 9M4WSB as the permanent station call sign. All was ready in time for the 57th JOTA.

The 57th JOTA 2014

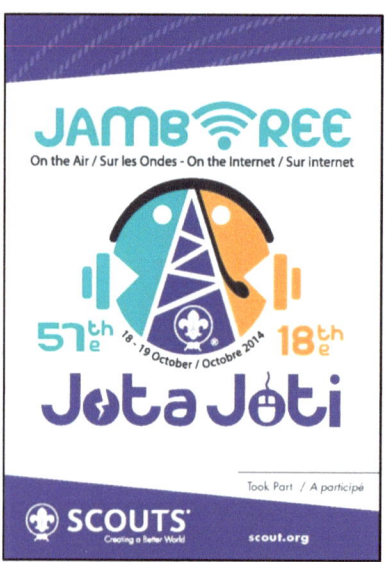

This year something different happened…..

2014 saw a large number of changes and improvements introduced to the JOTA-JOTI event.

In July, I presented JOTA-JOTI to the World Scout Conference in Ljubljana, triggering a lot of interest. Little did I know at the time, it would be the start of JOTA-JOTI presentations at several other WOSM World events.

Just before the JOTA-JOTI weekend, at 6 October 2014, I received the sad news that the founding father of the Jamboree on the Air, Mr Leslie Mitchell (91), had gone home. In memory of Les, all stations world-wide had 1 minute radio- and internet silence on 18 October at 12:00 UTC. I managed to attend his funeral, directly after the JOTA-JOTI weekend to represent WOSM.

The WJJT introduced new games for Scouts to play with and try out. We had "Sinbad's travels" around the globe. A new version of the bingo game "JamPuz" was presented, as well as several on-line challenges that could be entered on our new Facebook page. A webchat provided by Scoutlink was integrated into the new web site, and so were direct links to JOTI-radio. Scouts could take part in the Digital Campfire presented by JOTI.tv.

The World Scout Bureau staff and volunteers operated the newly established

Richard Middelkoop

station 9M4WSB from Port Dickson, south of Kuala Lumpur. Radio station HB9S operated from the Satigny Scout centre near Geneva and was henceforth supported by the European Regional Office. Yves Margot remained in function as the station manager.

The new JamPuz game (a sort of bingo game where one needs to collect codes) remained popular as ever.

The 58th JOTA 2015

Together with my XYL and the staff of the Jamboree's amateur radio station, I ran a JOTA-JOTI promotion stand at the 23rd World Scout Jamboree in Japan. We received many curious visitors, and were honoured by a visit of the Crown Prince of Japan.

New offered JOTA-JOTI programmes included "The Goals", an education and learning portal on sustainable development by UNESCO, WOSM and Lund University. The Digital Campfire by JOTI.tv now included a live Scout video-chat facility.

The World Scout Bureau operated 9M4WSB from the office in Kuala Lumpur, with many Scout visitors from the city and region, whilst I celebrated my personal 40th JOTA with the local Scout group in Nijkerk, The Netherlands this year.

On-line chat subjects in Canada included the use of alternative fuels, favorite movies, citizenship requirements, school work and a discussion about a fox getting into a chicken coop in Australia and stealing a chicken. The Cyprus Guides Association invited their members from all over Cyprus to sleep-over at their main offices in Nicosia.

In Estonia, Scouts did a training on "Internet security for kids". One Scout group gathered to have a Scout camp indoors. They had real tents

Temporary antennas for 9M4WSB on top of the World Scout Bureau office building, downtown Kuala Lumpur.

CQ Jamboree

Girl-Scouts manage to get on the air as well..

indoors with computers in tents. Luxemburg focused this year on SSTV; interesting images ex-changed between the groups. A huge increase of participation in Malaysia; the result of the role played by amateur radio operators during the big flood end of last year.

Namibia: "we all had a weekend with a lot of fun.... The only thing that came too short was sleep....!"

The opening speech at LA4JAM in Norway was given by the Norwegian International Commissioner Henrik Vagle Dalsgaard. A Rovers team in Portugal had an interesting adventure climbing a mountain and activating a SOTA (summit on the air) reference. On Saturday night, the Senegalese campfire was followed live via skype by Scouts in Bordeaux, France.

A few more changes....

During the course of 2015 and early 2016, the World JOTA-JOTI Team (WJJT) managed a few more adaptions to the JOTA-JOTI organization. We were fortunate to have Stephen Peck appointed in KL as the new World Events director and our direct point of contact at the WSB Office. Steve brought his long Scout experience to the table, mixed with unrivaled British diplomacy. This was a tremendous improvement for our contacts with the WSB office staff. The World Scout Committee appointed Peter Blatch as our new Committee liaison, replacing Mari Nakano who needed to focus all her energy on the upcoming World Scout Jamboree in Japan. Peter gave us an energetic support for all aspects of the event and his enthusiasm is certainly very catching.

The WJJT focused on further integration of the event. A logical step was to ask all member Associations to henceforth appoint one National Co-ordinator for both JOTA and JOTI, as our direct point of contact.

The World JOTA-JOTI Team: (left to right) Jim Wilson, Hannu Råttö, Philip Bird, Ali al Mamari and Richard Middelkoop

Richard Middelkoop

This stimulated event integration at the national level and simplified a bit our communication demands.

Enter the trusted partners. The WJJT felt there must be a way to recognize partner teams and organizations that support the JOTA-JOTI event on a global level, to recommend their services to the JOTA-JOTI participants and to clearly distinguish them from other providers. So the trusted-partner scheme was born. The team established basic entry criteria and a distinctive logo was made for use on the web sites of the trusted partners. We started with two partners, Scoutlink and JOTI.tv. The trusted-partner scheme is meant to grow over the coming years.

Since we now used an on-line sign-up system for the event, coupled to the WOSM web site scout.org, it appeared no longer possible for WAGGGS guide units to enter into the event. Whilst there have not been any official JOTA- or JOTI organized activities by our sister organization, guide units were known to frequently take part in the event. Upon the team's suggestion, the World Scout Committee consulted with her WAGGGS counterparts. It was decided to allow guide units to directly sign-up for and participate in the JOTA-JOTI event without the need to liaise with a WOSM group first. At least for the coming 3 years and to be evaluated after that. So we created a unique situation for a WOSM World Event. Perhaps another example of "connecting Scouts (and Guides)"?

Furthermore, I asked the WSB Regional support centres, as they were now called, to actively engage in the event. The Europe support centre kindly offered to continue to run HB9S from Geneva on their behalf.

The 59th JOTA 2016

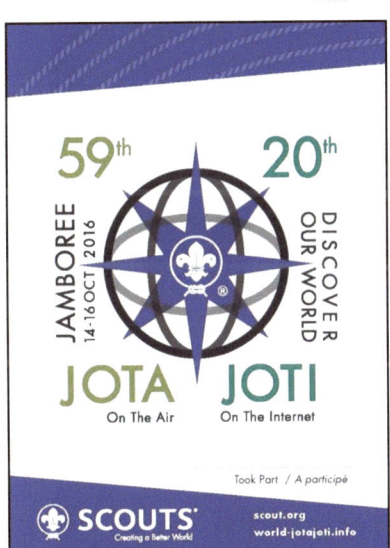

June, July and August, promotion time for JOTA-JOTI. Jim Wilson was present at the Dayton Hamvention in the US and I visited the radio station at the Roverway camp in Jambville near Paris. The WJJT launched a bi-weekly team blog on the event web site.

One troop in Canada talked with U.K. scouts on Skype; they took a picture of the screen at the same time as their interlocutors did on their own screen. Scouts in Curaçao were live the whole Saturday via an internet television system that was broadcasted in The Netherlands, where Scouts created an electronics kit in the form of a windmill with flashing leds.

The Scoutlink Country Coordinator for Italy, Ciro Attanasio, married during the JOTA-JOTI with all JOTA-JOTI participants in Italy virtually present.

The first snow for the winter season precipitates during the JOTA-JOTI weekend in Norway. Participating Scout groups experienced cold, snowing weather. Exceptionally nice weather in Tunisia, allowing outdoor activities. The participants discovered amateur radio, had workshops to build wire antennas, digital communications, computer networking, robotics and Arduino-based electronics.

CQ Jamboree

The president of Sudan Scout Association announced technical Scouts as new group branch, to play a role in emergency support. A Scout group from Kyiv, Ukraine, contacted the World Scout Seminar on the 'Messengers of Peace' using Skype. Scouts in the United States learned is that it is very common for people in other countries to speak multiple languages. And that other Scouting organizations have co-ed groups.

At the World Scout Bureau in Kuala Lumpur, I worked with a team of local radio amateurs and station manager Zakran Manan to set up temporary antennas, all the way on top of the building on the 20th floor. With the cables passing on the outside and entering the Bureau on the 17th floor where the main meeting room was converted into a radio operator room for 9M4S. The Malaysian authorities granted us the "S" call sign for special events, so we could use it for JOTA-JOTI. We used the excellent internet facilities of the Bureau to run the on-line activities.

Fun with connecting computers.

The 60th JOTA 2017

Early June, 21 National JOTA-JOTI Coordinators from all over the globe, met in Tallinn, Estonia for the 10th Radio Scouting and Internet Seminar (RSIS). In July, the World Scout Moot in Iceland hosted TF15MOOT and I ran a JOTA-JOTI promotion stand at the WOSM centre of the camp.

A JOTA-JOTI promotion video was shown at the World Scout Conference in Baku in August. For the first time since 1963, the Conference carried a number of official resolutions on JOTA-JOTI.

The new WOSM Secretary General Ahmad Alhendawi and several WSB staff joined the activities at 9M4S in October. Zakran and myself set up the station at a local school in Kuala Lumpur.

Participating Scout Umaibala told us, "my favourite is communicating with others using the radio. You cannot see their face when you speak to them which is a little bit weird and you don't know who is there!". Over 300 Scouts enjoyed the various workshops. Quite a happening.

Bolivia boosted participation from 5 to 24%. And a 120% increase in Colombian JOTA-JOTI participation this year. Estonian Scouts had extremely funny contacts with "GB2GP" at Gilwell park.

Richard Middelkoop

And Scouts in Greece were amazed that groups from different places on the globe were communicating as if they were right next door!

Italian astronaut Paolo Nespoli IZ0JPA was happy to talk with Italian Scouts from the International Space Station (ISS). It was the highlight of the weekend. The Scouts of Lebanon organized their first JOTA-JOTI, after many years.

Four young ladies operated the Namibian Jamboree Station V55JOTA and the radio world went nuts!!! Pileup after pileup; everyone wanted to talk to one of these girls.

Secretary General Ahmad Alhendawi studying Jampuz with Scouts at 9M4S in Kuala Lumpur.

Scouts at LA8GMA in Norway selected the tallest spruce tree around for their antenna; and used a remote radio-controlled drone to place their antenna up to the tree-top! Scouts in Dnipro, Ukraine, occupied a whole room in a local café to use a good wifi, and to show what Scouting is to the café's guests.

Introducing new friends to the magic of JOTA-JOTI.

Just after the JOTA-JOTI weekend, on 15 December 2017, I received the sad news that the first World JOTA Organizer, Mr Len F Jarrett (96), VE3MYF, had gone home.

I had kept in contact with Len over the years and visited him in Ottawa as my QRL brought me to Canada a few times. In fact, our last contact was about preparing this updated booklet. Condolence letters from his former WSB collegues and the current WOSM Secretary General were sent to his family.

Len Jarrett, VE3MYF
SK 2017

CQ Jamboree

The World Scout Bureau station

Ever since the first JOTA, the World Scout Bureau operated an amateur radio station. As Len has written in the first part of this book, at first the Bureau used private stations, later on it acquired its own call sign. From VE3JAM and VE3WSB to HB9S and now to 9M4WSB and 9M4S. I did some research through the old notes and reports and was able to compile an overview of the World Bureau's amateur

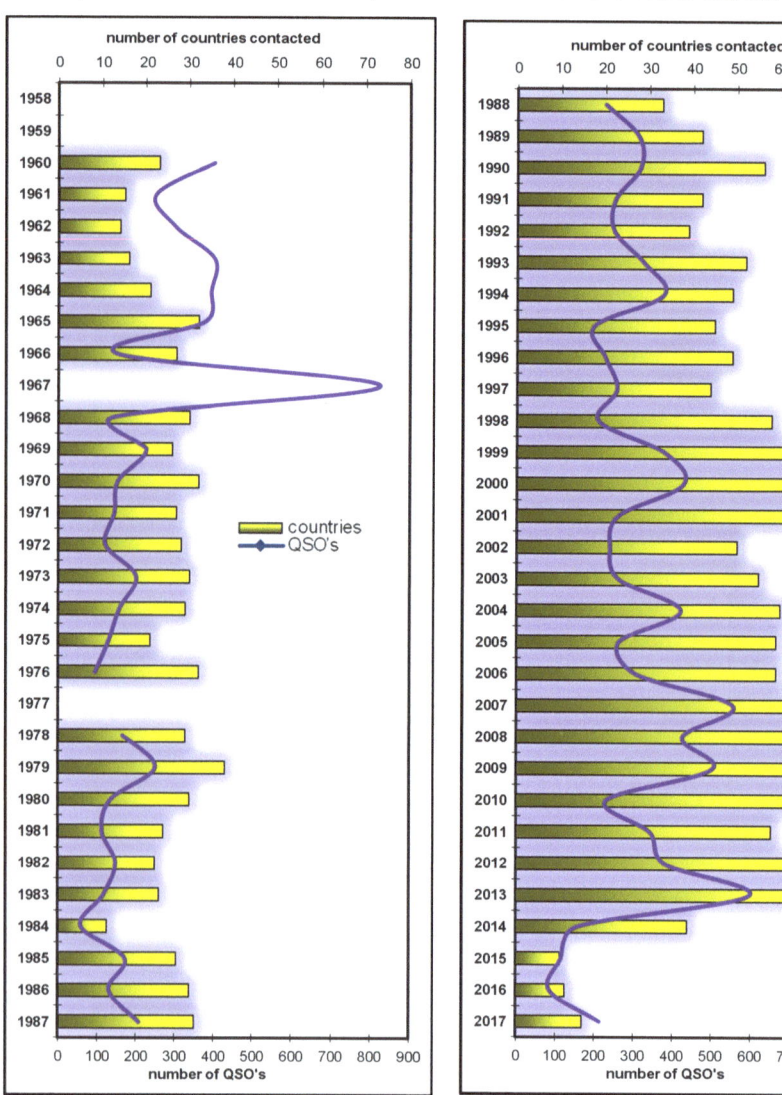

World Scout Bureau's amateur radio station activity overview.

radio activity. For the last decade or so, this was relatively easy, as the HB9S station manager Yves Margot kept an excellent record of all details. Documentation from the earlier years, however, was more difficult to obtain, as many archives were lost when the Bureau moved from one place to another and experienced subsequent clean-up activities as well. Of course, the latter is inevitable, otherwise the office space in Kuala Lumpur would by now be fully filled with JOTA archive material.

JOTA is not about numbers of course. It is about friendship, making contacts and feeling part of a world-wide movement. Yet we need some numbers to make the activities visible. The graph shows all the JOTA's that the World Scout Bureau has been active in with an amateur radio station.

The graph shows the number of countries in which Scouts were contacted and the number of radio contacts (QSO's) that we had in a JOTA weekend, from 1958 up to 2017. There is no data unfortunately, of the first two JOTA's.

Some interesting details to know: the Bureau has actually operated in only 59 JOTA's; in 1977 Len Jarrett went to The Netherlands and did not operate a World Scout Bureau station.

Very distinct is the one JOTA that coincided with the World Scout Jamboree in 1967; the World Scout Bureau used the Jamboree station K7WSJ and made many more contacts than usual.

Since the 1990's, the number of contacted countries started to grow. For two reasons: after clear political changes, Scouting was restarted in many Eastern-European countries. And HB9S started to operate with a larger international team of Scout radio amateurs.

I had the pleasure to operate HB9S myself from 1987 to 2014, in the first years occasionally just with the two of us (station manager Yves Margot and myself), mostly hosted at the facilities of the Geneva amateur radio club, on the attic of a primary school in Petit Lancy, a Geneva suburb.

But more recently with a larger team. Each year with different Scout amateurs, mostly from Europe. With the station set up at the Swiss Scout Centre Les Pérouses, in Satigny, a few kilometers outside Geneva.

Occasionally, Yves and I ventured elsewhere, like Tilehurst, UK for the 40th JOTA, Froideville near Lausanne with a local Swiss group, or to the Collex radio club, north of Geneva.

The start-up of 9M4S in Malaysia, after the move of the World Scout Bureau in 2014, was small. A new local team had to be formed by the new station manager Zakran Abdul Manan and each year another location was tried, including the office building itself in 2015 and 2016. I felt the operation in 2017 from the premises of a local school, was the best one yet, as we could accommodate many young Scouts and offer several workshops.

You can also see that indeed the years in Ottawa (before this large World Scout Jamboree peak) more contacts were made than initially at the start in Geneva (after the Jamboree peak) as Len already mentioned earlier. We see a similar effect now after the move to Kuala Lumpur. A contact with the World Scout Bureau station has once more become a most wanted, rare DX occasion...

CQ Jamboree

The World Scout Bureau amateur radio station operated for the JOTA from:

JOTA	year	Call sign	QTH	JOTA	year	Call sign	QTH
1	1958	VE3RT	Ottawa	31	1988	HB9S	Pt. Lancy
2	1959	VE3GI	Ottawa	32	1989	HB9S	Pt. Lancy
3	1960	VE3JAM	Connaught Ranges	33	1990	HB9S	Pt. Lancy
4	1961	VE3JAM	Connaught Ranges	34	1991	**HE7S**	Pt. Lancy
5	1962	VE3WSB	Connaught Ranges	35	1992	HB9S	Perouses
6	1963	VE3WSB	WSB Ottawa	36	1993	HB9S	Pt. Lancy
7	1964	VE3WSB	WSB Ottawa	37	1994	HB9S	Pt. Lancy
8	1965	VE3WSB	WSB Ottawa	38	1995	HB9S	Pt. Lancy
9	1966	VE3WSB	WSB Ottawa	39	1996	HB9S	Pt. Lancy
10	1967	**K7WSJ**	WSJ Idaho	40	1997	**GB/HB9S**	Tilehurst
11	1968	**4U1ITU**	Geneva	41	1998	HB9S	Pt. Lancy
12	1969	**4U1ITU**	Geneva	42	1999	HB9S	Pt. Lancy
13	1970	HB9S	WSB Geneva	43	2000	**HB2S**	Perouses
14	1971	HB9S	WSB Geneva	44	2001	HB9S	Perouses
15	1972	HB9S	Mt Chasseron	45	2002	HB9S	Froideville
16	1973	HB9S	Mt Chasseron	46	2003	HB9S	Collex + Kalkar
17	1974	HB9S	WSB Geneva	47	2004	HB9S	WSB +Collex
18	1975	HB9S	WSB Geneva	48	2005	HB9S	WSB +Collex
19	1976	HB9S	WSB Geneva	49	2006	HB9S	Perouses
20	1977		Not operated	50	2007	**HB50S**	Perouses
21	1978	HB9S	Perouses	51	2008	HB9S	Perouses
22	1979	**HB7S**	Perouses	52	2009	**HE8S**	Perouses
23	1980	**GB2WSB**	Datchet	53	2010	HB9S	Perouses
24	1981	HB9S	WSB Geneva	54	2011	HB9S	Perouses
25	1982	HB9S	WSB Geneva	55	2012	HB9S	Perouses
26	1983	HB9S	WSB Geneva	56	2013	HB9S	Perouses
27	1984	HB9S	WSB Geneva	57	2014	9M4WSB	Port Dickson
28	1985	HB9S	Perouses	58	2015	9M4WSB	WSB Kuala Lumpur
29	1986	HB9S	Perouses	59	2016	9M4S	WSB Kuala Lumpur
30	1987	HB9S	Perouses	60	2017	9M4S	Kuala Lumpur

Richard Middelkoop

The World Scout Bureau amateur radio station operated from different locations for the JOTA over the years:

> Connaught Ranges: an army compound just outside Ottawa, Canada.
> The World Scout Jamboree in Farragut State park, Idaho, USA.
> The United Nations ITU amateur radio station in Geneva, Switzerland.
> Mt Chasseron: a mountain location in the Swiss Alps.
> Les Pérouses: a Swiss Scout centre in Satigny, near Geneva, Switzerland.
> Datchet: a village near the hometown of Les Mitchell at the time.
> Petit Lancy: home of the Geneva radio club HB9G in a Geneva suburb.
> The 1st Reading Scout group in Tilehurst United Kingdom.
> Froideville: a former air traffic beacon house near Lausanne, Switzerland.
> Collex: home of the Geneva radio club HB9UU, north of Geneva.
> Kalkar: a DPSG international Scout meeting centre, Germany.
> Port Dickson: a resort south of Kuala Lumpur, Malaysia.
> WSB: the actual office building or the World Scout Bureau in Ottawa, Geneva and Kuala Lumpur.

JAMBOREE-ON-THE-AIR

WORLD-WIDE SCOUTING friendships will be extended by everybody who takes part in the 5th Jamboree-on-the-Air. This year's broadcast of friendship will begin Greenwich mean time at 0000 October 20 (Saturday) and end at 2400 October 21 (Sunday).

Anyone who is not an amateur radio operator (ham) may arrange with a nearby ham or radio club to be put on the air. All participants must strictly observe their national license regulations as explained by the host ham.

The jamboree will be held on five bands: 10, 15, 20, 40, and 80 meters. Either code or voice transmission may be used. Enter the event by calling "CQ Jamboree" or by answering a station you hear giving this call.

The Boy Scouts World Bureau sponsors this annual Jamboree-on-the-Air and operates its own station, VE3WSB —V E 3 World Scout Bureau. K2BFW, the BOYS' LIFE Amateur Radio Club station will also be on the air on frequencies adjacent to those listed and also on 3.560 kc., 7.050 kc., and 14.110 kc. VE3WSB will operate on the following frequencies, depending upon conditions: 10 meter band, 28,490 kc. to 28,510 kc.; 15 meter band, 21,195 kc. to 21,210 kc.*; 20 meter band, 14.195 kc. (listening also on 14,210)*;

40 meter band, 7,250 kc.; 80 meter band, 3,760 kc. and 3,820 kc.**

* On these bands, VE3WSB will give preference to stations outside Canada and the U.S.A. at all times.

** The lower frequency will be used during the *odd* hours GMT for Canadian stations; the higher frequency during the *even* hours for U.S.A. stations; *except* from 0100-0300 GMT and 1300-1500 on both days, lower frequency will be used for CW contacts with U.S.A. novices.

QSL cards for reports of a contact with VE3WSB will be handled by the BOYS' LIFE Amateur Radio Club. In addition, the club will QSL all contacts and SWL reports for K2BFW.

Reports should include the following information: *Time*—use GMT, which is 5 hours ahead of Eastern standard time; *Station Heard*—give call letters; *Phone-CW*; *QSO*—briefly describe the conversation heard; *Frequency*—list the frequency as near as possible in either kilocycles or megacycles; *RST* —tell whether signal was strong or not and if the conversation was easily readable.

Address QSL cards for VE3WSB and K2BFW to Boys' LIFE Radio Club, B.S.A., New Brunswick. N. J.

The first mention of VE3WSB in the leaders magazine "Scouting" of the Boy Scouts of America, October 1962.

CQ Jamboree

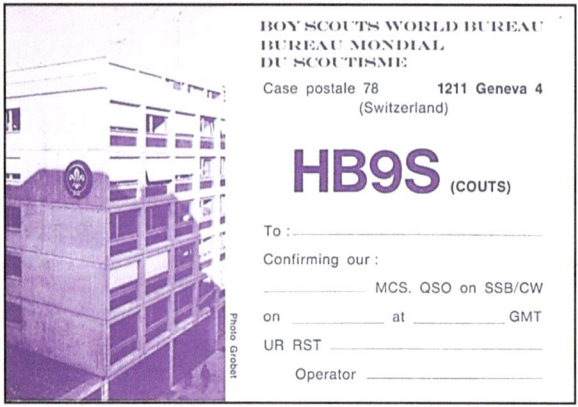

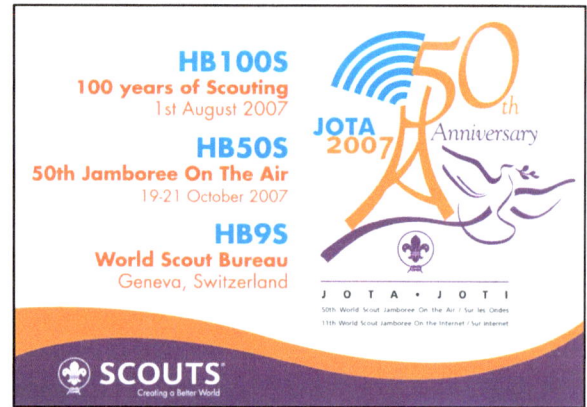

Some of the many QSL cards that the World Scout Bureau used over the years.

Richard Middelkoop

JOTA Reports and stories

For some reason, Scouters seem reluctant to send in reports of their participation - this problem is not, of course, peculiar to JOTA. National Organizers have devised various methods to overcome the problems on a national level and some have met with success. One Australian state, for example, claims 93% response. The Netherlands goes one step better; by agreement with the government, Scouts are allowed to speak on the air provided their station has registered with Scout H.Q. beforehand. On the world level, only about half the countries taking part send in reports to the Bureau. From these, one can discover others and thus obtain a reasonable estimate of the number of countries participating and, sometimes, an idea of the number of stations together with the total number of participants.

The Bureau continued to promote the idea of each Scout Association appointing a National Organizer, preferably a Scouter holding a radio licence, and, by 1970, there were about 50 of these with whom the Bureau could communicate directly. Of course, regular channels were not neglected, but this Organizer network gave us an additional means, not only of "spreading the word" but, also, of obtaining reliable reports.

It was as a consequence of this that the Bureau was able to provide the first reliable participation statistics in the early 1970's - "6,000 stations in over 70 countries" and a total participation of "around 200,000 Scouts and Girl Guides".

"Exact participation numbers are anybody's guess" was a comment Len wrote in various World JOTA Reports. I have gone again through the reports of the past JOTA's, collecting all the reliable information I could find. From the start up to 1988, 11 World JOTA Reports present the number of participating stations, based on an estimate and on the details received from various countries. Using a logarithmic regression technique and a computer, I estimated the numbers for the other years. These numbers agree very well with the various estimates given in the respective World Reports.

The first world JOTA report was published in 1961.

In 1989, I introduced a report form for National JOTA Organizers that also asked for some participation numbers in their country. So now the Bureau had more accurate information available. From the reports, I could calculate the average participation per country. Using a mathematical technique, I could also apply this average to the countries that did not sent a report but were known to be active in the JOTA because they were mentioned in the reports of others. And since the Bureau knew the exact membership number in each country, it wasn't hard to compute the best estimate of the total JOTA participation. In fact, this technique is still in use today.

The following figure shows the number of countries reported active in the JOTA. Quite quickly after the start of the JOTA, the event had spread to almost all the countries that had Scout organizations. On average some 80 countries were represented up to the early nineties of the last century. The graph clearly shows

CQ Jamboree

the increase in participating countries in the early 2000's, due to the participation of eastern-European countries. The average increased to around 110 countries and got another boost from 2002 onwards when Echolink was introduced to the JOTA. This brought the average number of participating countries up to around 150 each year.

The way that JOTI participation was reported in the past, however, differed from the JOTA statistics. To have a consistent overview, I have interpolated the JOTI numbers from the available data and shown them in the graph. From 2014 onwards, JOTA-JOTI is one event and the graph shows the combined numbers only.

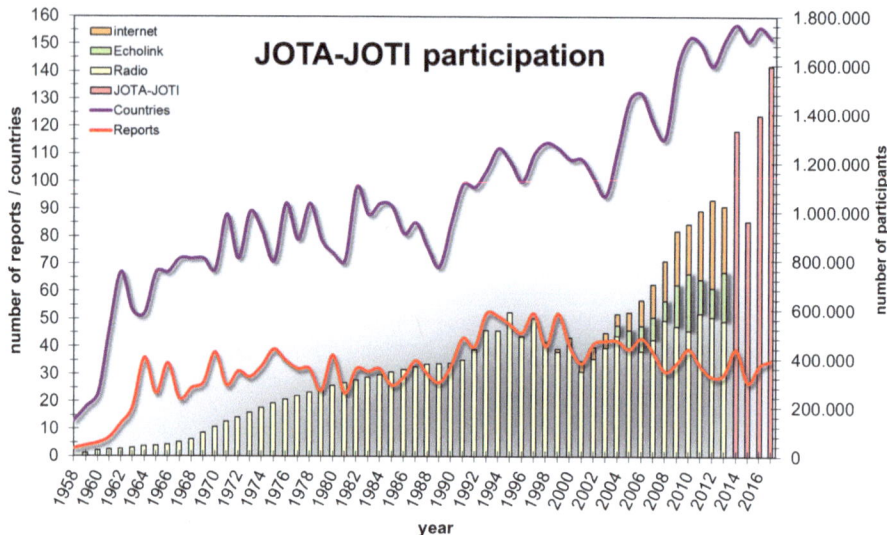

In 2015, we had a newer sign-up system in place that decided to become disfunctional and simply stopped working on the Saturday morning of the JOTA-JOTI weekend. A slight drop in the number of received National Reports, didn't help either that year. Hence this large dip in participation statistics. We could have extrapolated the numbers manually, but that would be more guess work rather than calculations, so this is what we have.

Reporting back to the World Scout Bureau is a different story; on several occasions 50 per cent of all participating countries sent a report. The average, however, is that around 35 percent sends a report to the World Scout Bureau. This has been a fairly stable number during the past years.

As you can see from these graphs, JOTA has steadily grown since its inception in 1958. Together with the JOTI, it reaches a participation level of well above a million Scouts each year. Except for a curious and unexplained dip in 2001 (was it the sunspot cycle, the massive introduction of computers or simply a miscalculation in several reports?), participation has been fairly stable. Of course, each year new Scouts and Girl Guides are introduced to amateur radio and internet and exchange friendship over the airwaves. I wonder how many it might have been in total since the start in 1958?

Richard Middelkoop

Amateur Radio at World Scout Jamborees

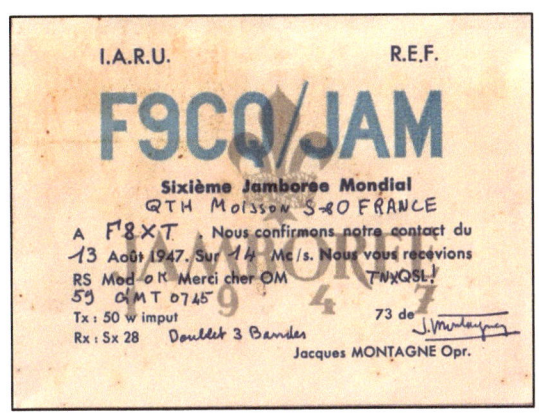

The 6th World Scout Jamboree was held in Moisson, France in 1947, directly after World War II. Radio technology had developed quickly during the years of the war. No doubt, there was a great emphasis on re-uniting people after these difficult years. Through recent research, I discovered that the "Jamboree de la Paix" (Jamboree of Peace) hosted an amateur radio station on its camp site, which was not well-known so far. This is actually the first occasion that an amateur radio station operated from a World Scout Jamboree.

For the first time ever, Scouts could communicate with others not present at the camp itself using the equipment of F9CQ/JAM. The station was run by Jacques Montagne of the "Réseau des Émitteurs Français" (REF). He was able to establish contact with 9 different countries, as far away as the USA, Brazil, Venezuela, Costa Rica, Saudi Arabia and Australia. All with a 50 W transmitter on a dipole antenna, strung between the trees on the campsite.

In the "Radio Ref" magazine of November 1947, Jacques writes: "we discovered that Scouts and Radio Amateurs share the same ideals, to help each other, serve their country, develop friendships between men with no distinction on race, religion or opinion, to ensure peace". And "I hope that this first participation of an amateur radio station in a large happening will be repeated in the future."

So it became clear what a good match there is between Scouts and Radio Amateurs. This operation laid the basis for what was to submerge a few year later, the idea for the largest youth gathering on earth, the Jamboree-On-The-Air. Jacques' hopes came true, as you will see on the next pages.

At the 7th World Scout Jamboree in Bad Ischl, Austria, local radios were in use by the Scouts, as the newspaper mentioned: "the French have equipped

CQ Jamboree

their headquarters with great elegance, their own dynamo system even provides electric light, and their own telephone lines and ringer radios connect with their squads throughout the camp."

The camp newspaper also mentions shortwave radio transmissions around the globe with news from the camp. Provided by the "red-white-red radio team", using a mobile studio and portable tape recorder.

I have not found any evidence of amateur radio at the 8th _World Scout Jamboree_ in Niagara, Canada in 1955. It is known, however, that the Canadian Broadcasting Corporation did broadcast both AM and shortwave from the Jamboree, simulcasting on CBS Radio in the US, and this coverage was also retransmitted on the Voice of America on shortwave. Also, live television coverage was provided. The Jamboree report pictures the CBC transmission tower.

The CBC transmission tower at the Jamboree.

(Len Jarrett continues his personal account)

The 1957 station GB3SP has already been described by Les Mitchell in his introduction and, although I was present at the 9th _World Scout Jamboree_, I did not have the opportunity to visit the station. However, since part of my duties with the World Bureau involved attendance at world events, I was fortunate to see and usually operate the radio station at every World Jamboree between 1959 and 1983, and was involved in the organization of several.

The GB3SP Jamboree station.

Richard Middelkoop

The station DU1PAR at the *10th World Scout Jamboree*, at Makiling Park, Philippines, was a very modest setup by recent standards, but nevertheless was very efficient and attracted a lot of attention. At that time, I did not, of course, hold a licence and could not, therefore, operate it.

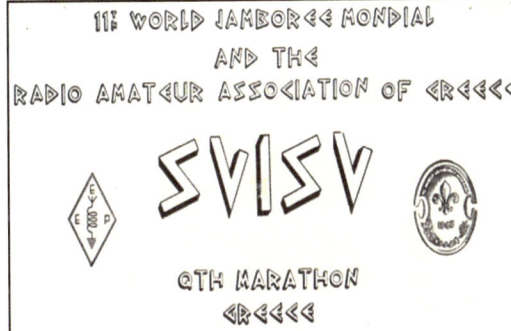

But I was able to operate the station SV1SV at the *11th World Scout Jamboree* in Greece in 1963, and to experience for the first time the famous "European QRM" I had heard so much about. Little did I know then that some five years later, it was to become my permanent "milieu". Here again, it was quite a modestly equipped station, but was staffed by an enthusiastic team of operators and was very popular.

The official souvenir book of the Jamboree features SV1SV in action.

CQ Jamboree

The *12th World Scout Jamboree's* radio station, K7WSJ, in Idaho, USA, in 1967, set the pattern for the more elaborate setups which were to become the pattern. There were actually several complete stations, all operating from a large marquee using separate antennas. I was pleased to have time to do some operating from this station, particularly as the 10th JOTA had been scheduled for the same dates and K7WSJ was, as a consequence, the World Bureau's official station. This Jamboree was the first to have "link camps" set up around the world during the same period, many of them with radio stations. Perhaps the most notable was the one at Brownsea Island, in the south of England, "where it all began". K7WSJ had a daily schedule with GB3BSI during the run of the Jamboree.

Shelly Weil, K2BS, calls CQ over shortwave radio from Idaho.

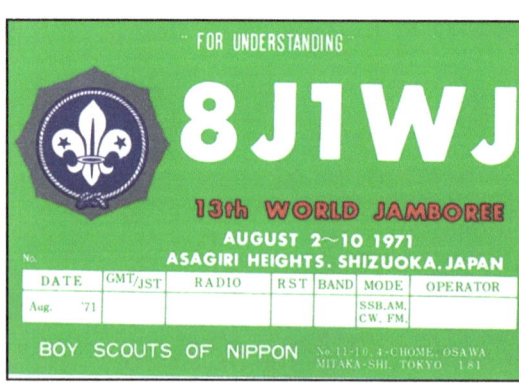

In 1971, the *13th World Scout Jamboree* was held on the slopes of Mount Fuji, Japan and, as might be expected in the "home of the transistor" the Boy Scouts of Japan had set up a veritable "antenna farm" of six separate stations, all operating under the very distinctive and popular call sign of 8J1WJ. The Jamboree was struck by a typhoon, but the station managed to keep going throughout. Here again, I managed to find some time to do some operating.

Richard Middelkoop

The impressive antenna farm of 8J1WJ

But it was left to the Scandinavians to really show us "how it should be done" when they organized LC1J from the <u>14th World Scout Jamboree</u> at Lillehammer, in Norway, in 1975. With an international team of operators, the area included not only several operating stations, using all modes, including CW, Radiotelephony, RTTY and Satellite Communication, but also a slide show, fox hunting and kit building.

Station Manager Tom-Victor Segalstad, LA4LN writes: one story about the monster wire beam pointing West (to America). I was testing the beam with 5 elements on 40 m after we put it up, at fairly low power, just to check the SWR. I said "this is LC1J testing". And a strong voice came out of the loudspeaker: "Who is testing on this frequency? this is OA ...". Well, I had to tell him that I was sorry if I interrupted some QSO over there in Peru, South America, but I had listened prior to testing, and the frequency sounded clear to me. "Yes, the frequency is clear -- I just wanted to report that you have the strongest signal on the band with 10 dB over S9 here in Peru".

LC1J under canvas at the 14th World Scout Jamboree in Lillehamar, Norway.

CQ Jamboree

A JOTA Conference during the Jamboree produced some very interesting suggestions from the 40 or so Radio-Scouts present.

The Iranians had planned an elaborate station for the 15th World Jamboree which had been scheduled to be held there in 1979 and I had been involved in the planning. Unfortunately, as is well known, the Jamboree had to be cancelled at the last moment.

By 1983 I had returned to Canada and was enlisted in the planning of the station VE6WSJ at the _15th World Scout Jamboree_ near Calgary. This was the most ambitious one yet, with a whole area of radios, televisions, computers, satellite communication and kit building. The theme was "Communication" and visitors were taken by members of the international staff through the exhibit, starting with primitive communications, through telephones, radios, TVs, teletype to computers. The final exhibit, with about 20 computers to play with, was the most popular.

The antenna array of VE6WSJ was most impressive with a 6-element HF beam and even a 2-element 40m beam.

(continued by Richard Middelkoop)

The _16th World Scout Jamboree_ took place in 1988 in Australia. A permanent building at Cataract Scout Park housed the amateur radio station AX2SWJ and I was privileged to be part of the radio staff, like I had been on the previous World Jamboree in Canada. This time, together with my YL Miriam who functioned as the station's receptionist. With separate antennas for each amateur

Richard Middelkoop

AX2SWJ in its permanent housing at Cataract Park.

band many contacts were made throughout the world.

The Governor General of Australia visited the station and was impressed with the sked board which showed many prearranged contacts with foreign Scout stations or with relatives of Scouts present at the Jamboree.

Despite the solar minimum, which limited radio propagation, many interesting contacts were made. Especially the one we made for a Scout from New Zealand, whose parents lived in the outback and had no telephone. We found a radio amateur close by who moved his entire station to the parent's home and made contact. The parents received a lively report from their son at the Jamboree.

An exposition which featured old and new radio equipment and an instruction session about radio operation also received lots of attention from the nearly 300 visiting Scouts each day.

In 1991 the *17th World Scout Jamboree* was on the air from Mt. Soraksan National Park in South-Korea with the station 6K17WJ. The less favourable antenna situation, close to power lines, did not keep us from making a few contacts with Scout stations far away. The 80 m and 40 m band transceivers were surplus army equipment and quite fun to operate.

I also managed several DX contacts on the more modern equipment that Shelly, K2BS, brought along with him from the US. The majority of contacts were made with Japan. We were particularly pleased with the almost daily contact with Father Moran, 9N1MM, who was the only radio amateur in Nepal and associated with the Scout group which was present at the Jamboree.

The international part of the radio staff was quite small, and the staff meetings in Korean were quite challenging to us. Luckily we had "miss Kim" to translate it all.

The Morse-code instruction also attracted the attention of Secretary General Jacques Moreillon, who knew how to operate the key. An electronic flashing badge was built by Scouts during the kit building session. Unfortunately, South-Korea ran out of batteries, so we could only test a few.

CQ Jamboree

The entrance gate of 6K17WJ where we welcomed a few hundred Scouts each morning.

The 18th *World Scout Jamboree* took place in The Netherlands in 1995 and attracted 29.000 Scouts from 169 different countries. I had the pleasure to be the station manager and was involved in all of the Jamboree preparations. Scouts at the Jamboree spoke directly with their friends at home, via the radio. PA6WSJ made 3145 short-wave radio contacts to 137 different countries in all parts of the world. It transmitted television pictures of the World Scout Jamboree too!

The Croatian contingent had it all worked out: they asked a radio amateur at their home town to listen for the radio transmissions from the Jamboree. At a prearranged time, the contingent visited the station. They were put in touch directly with their friends at home. What a surprise to hear that several of the boy's parents had come to the station! Amateur Radio, was one of their highlights at the Jamboree.

Among the many stations contacted was the one of His Majesty King Hussein of Jordan. King Hussein operated his own amateur radio station, JY1, and had been looking to get into contact with the World Scout Jamboree for several days, since his sister was present at the opening ceremony.

David and Ruben, both Scouts from South-Africa, walked in one day and asked if they could speak to their home

Richard Middelkoop

country, only to find their hometown group, White River Scouts, with their leader Jenny on the air, within minutes after the first CQ.

Scouts could choose from activities like time-zone calculation, computer logging of contacts, a six-position short wave reception station, a do-it-yourself antenna workshop and a Morse-code competition.

Slow-scan television pictures (SSTV), taken from a camera on top of the Jamboree's record tower at a height of 35 metres, were transmitted via short-wave radio. The world could see "the view from above".

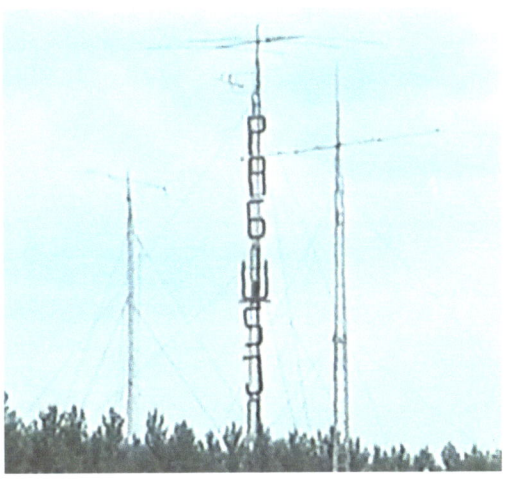

From well below to well above sea level: the antenna farm of PA6WSJ.

Scouts could send and receive messages via a computer connected to the international packet-radio network. The biggest thrill was to receive an answer delivered to their sub camp as an official "Jamboree radio telegram".

At the "Scoutronic" workshop Scouts constructed their own electronic Dutch windmill with flashing lights. All 4500 kits were sold out at the end of the camp.

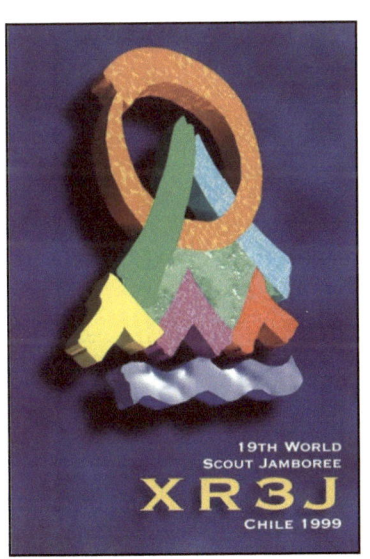

The _19th World Scout Jamboree_ brought together 30.000 Scouts in 1999 in Picarquin, Chile, at a beautiful camp site at the foot of the Andes mountains. As early as 1996, the camp director Patrick Lyon approached me with the question "could I please organize the Amateur Radio station for the Jamboree?" This turned out to be an exclusive international project where a team of Scout radio amateurs from 11 different countries offered an exciting programme. Special event station XR3J made 3759 radio contacts with 119 different countries around the world. 500 electronic kits were constructed, numerous SSTV pictures were transmitted, many messages were sent and / or received digitally. Our biggest technical challenge? Getting the equipment which we brought from various parts of the world (with different power plugs) to work on one set of Chilean power sockets.

Each participant received an amateur-radio-activity passport in English or Spanish with the activities he completed marked with a rubber stamp.

Many scouts enjoyed the possibility to speak on the radio themselves. During the first days of the Jamboree, many Scouts wanted to get a message home to their parents, but international phone calls were difficult from the camp site. XR3J had HF running and helped out. You should have seen the Scout's faces when we let them speak to their homes.

Short-wave receivers were set up to listen in to world-wide radio traffic and short-wave broadcast stations. Radio Mexico International included greeting messages for the Scouts at the Jamboree in a number of their programmes. Thousands of listeners around the world also heard these, which was good publicity.

The antennas of XR3J looking over the Andes at Picarquin.

We had the full capability to send and receive digital messages, even email worked via radio. The fox-hunt was truly international: the transmitters were built in The Netherlands, the receivers were from New Zealand and Finland. And it all worked together!

A computer ran a competition to find out who was the fastest to read Morse code letters. Some Scouts could decode Morse signals even faster than operators at our station.

The camp medical staff did call upon us to provide communications during the closing ceremony. The XR3J team managed to put all 5 first-aid posts on the air, staff a command post with bi-lingual communication to the ambulance service and provided a radio link to the camp hospital.

E20AJ was the "voice on the airwaves" of the *20th World Scout Jamboree* in Thailand in 2003. Operated by 31 staff members, 14 of them from outside Thailand, the station managed to make over 2000 contacts, in more than a hundred different countries. This time I was part of the World Scout Bureau's Jamboree support team and had other duties at the camp, looking after its entire Communications infrastructure. So I was not fully involved in the station, but managed to bring together an international operator team to support the Thai core team lead by khun Thida Denpruektham, HS1ASC. And I did some operating myself.

E20AJ was part of the Jamboree's City of Science, an area that offered all sorts of technical workshops, a.o. a 21st century foxhunt, to locate the mobile fox on the campsite. The fox played the tune "it's a small world after all", so we saw several Scouts dancing while they were trying to find the hidden fox transmitter…..

Two large tents and several beams: home of E20AJ at Sattahip, Thailand.

During one of the many radio contacts we were called by Roberto WA9E, from the USA. He asked us to please locate his daughter Laurne KB9DTE on the campsite for him. Could we please ask her to email a message home, as he hadn't heard from her yet? How do you find one person amongst another 20.000? Well, you contact the contingent and try your luck. We had her speak directly to her father over the radio two days later…..

An absolute highlight was the scheduled contact with the International Space Station, NA1SS. A thorough preparation had been done by Masashi, JI1CUJ and Chawalit, E21KEW. An automated antenna tracking system kept the double array of VHF beams pointed straight at the Spacecraft during its pass over Thailand. Together we did the final count down to the exact time that the spacecraft would be above the horizon. At precisely that moment the loudspeaker sounded out: "E20AJ this is NA1SS, how copy?" A loud applause filled the tent. For the next 10 minutes Scouts from various countries posed questions to Don Pettit, KD5MDT, the scientific officer on board the ISS.

The year 2007 was of course the highlight of it all. The 21st World Scout Jamboree in the United Kingdom hosted GB100J. Like at the previous Jamboree, I was responsible to support the entire ICT infrastructure of the camp on behalf of the World Scout Bureau and this limited my time at the amateur radio station. I did manage do stop by regularly though, and make an occasional QSO.

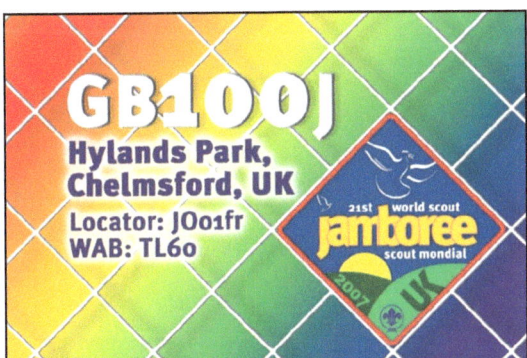

GB100J found itself in a large tent in an excellent location on the camp side, right in between the Global Development Village and the World Scout Centre. This meant lot's of visitors during day time and even at night. The international team of operators was lead by the UK National JOTA Organizer Richard Gaskell, G0REL. After some initial struggle to get all the equipment together and working, the only thing missing were the light bulbs. But there was no way to stop the enthusiastic operators. Yes,

CQ Jamboree

GB100J, in the large tent on the right, with its beam antennas.

you can ofcourse operate the short wave radio's at night and simply use a flashlight to read the station log....!

A daily contact was maintained with the amateur radio base at Brownsea Island GB100BI, with Gilwell Park GB2GP and with the reunion station at Sutton Coldfield GB4SP.

Two large beam antenna's plus a number of wire antennas in between the masts were the Jamboree's liveline with the outside world. An exciting foxhunt and a kit building project were there to complete the radio adventure for the participating Scouts.

Together with 120 Scout leaders from 86 different countries, I attended the 50th JOTA birthday party hosted by GB100J on August 4. A re-enactment of the amateur radio station from the Jubilee World Scout Jamboree, GB3SP in Sutton Coldfield in 1957 was displayed. Special guest was RSGB vice-president Colin Thomas G3PSM and his XYL. An excellent opportunity to exchange ideas amongst the Radio-Scouts of many nations. It was in the same informal atmosphere that the JOTA idea came up in 1957.

Ofcourse, no party without a birthday cake. The GB100J team had them specially made with the logo of the 50th JOTA on top. Symbolic for JOTA's rich history and future, I invited the most experienced Scout radio amateur on site, Tormod Nordeng, LA8RU, to cut the JOTA birthday cake together with the youngest Guide with a radio licence, Maura M3URA.

A contact was made on 4 August at 21:10 GMT with the International Space statio with astronaut Clay Anderson KD5PLA at the mike. Coordinated by Ivor G4GET, the uplink contact with NA1SS worked just perfectly. It was a clear night and not only could the Scouts speak with the Space station, they could also see it passing over in the sky above the Jamboree!!

Maura, M3URA and Tormod, LA8RU cut the 50th JOTA birthday cake.

Richard Middelkoop

1 August 2007: one World, one Promise, one Network

For the Sunrise Ceremony on Brownsea Island, I had organized a network of amateur radio stations at former World Scout Jamboree sites around the world. And quite a few other Centenary stations joined in as well. So this all became one big Scout radio network. I travelled down to Brownsea, away from the World Scout Jamboree for a few days, to assist with the Sunrise radio operations.

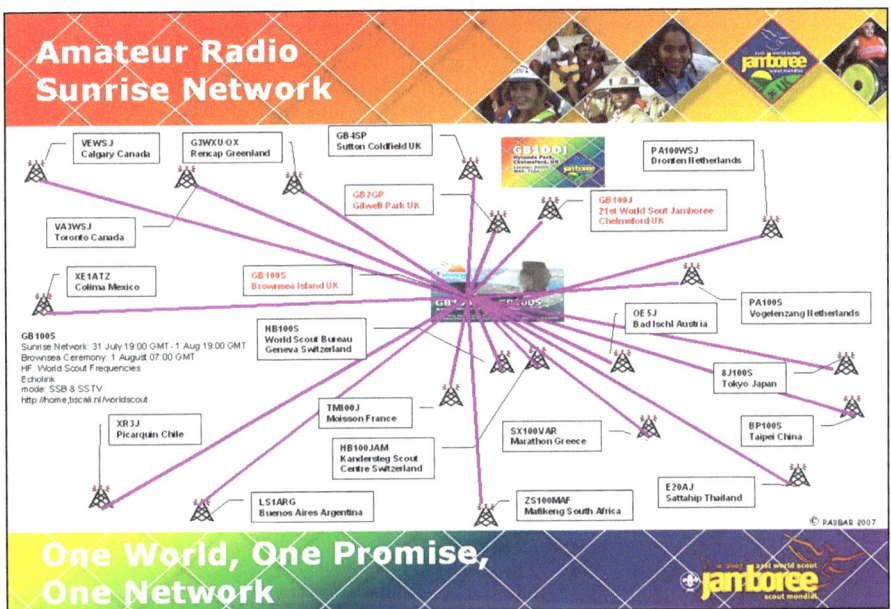

When the Sunrise of Scouting's new century commenced in Kiribati, messages started to come in to Brownsea via the radio. In Perth, Australia, the Brownsea replica camp set up on an island in the Swan river, was the first to send "happy birthday" greetings to Brownsea Island. Replica camp leader Steve said it was a great experience to Scouts camping in Bell tents. Western-Australia commissioner Liz remarked that feeling the atmosphere of friendship amongst the Scouts was the best experience to them all.

The amateur radio station at Brownsea was operating from battery power, as there is no electricity grid on the island. This meant that for each message transmitted, the Scouts cranked the energy from a generator bike. During good weather, they were helped by large solar panels. A wind generator bridged the days with less sunshine. The

CQ Jamboree

1 August 2007:
Sunrise at GB100S on Brownsea Island.

tallest point on the Island was the antenna mast of GB100S.

Station manager Frank Heritage, M0AEU and his international operator team did a super job in running the station, involving the Scouts in the contacts and making Brownsea the centre of Scouting for the day.

GB100S subsequently transmitted friendship messages from Scouts at Brownsea and recordings from the Sunrise Ceremony on the Island to the other Sunrise events around the world. 8J100S in Tokyo Japan, VR100S in Hong Kong, BP100S in Tapei Taiwan, PA100WSJ in Dronten The Netherlands, HB100J in Kandersteg Switzerland, HB100S at the World Scout Bureau Geneva, LS1ARG in Buenos Aires Argentina, XR3J at Picarquin Chile, TG100S in Guatemala and VE6WSJ in Calgary Canada were amongst the many contacts made. The Sunrise Ceremony in Calgary assembled many thousands of Scouts at the Olympic Bowl and played the friendship messages from Brownsea at the main stage. This really felt like a mini-JOTA, uniting the world by radio.

WOSM World Scout Committee vice-chairman Therese Bermingham and Secretary General Eduardo Missoni transmitted their personal messages to the world. Eduardo even sat a while on the generator bike, to crank enough energy for his message to be transmitted.

For the first time, Sweden was the host country for the 22<u>nd</u> _World Scout Jamboree_ in 2011. The World Scout Bureau support structure for world events had changed

since 2007, and this brought me into the planning team for the amateur radio activity. By coincidence, my regular job took me to Stockholm several times per year and this nicely combined with meetings of the planning team. From 27 July till 7 August 2011, the 22nd World Scout Jamboree was on the air with SJ22S. The station offered a full Radio-Scouting pro-gramme to the Jamboree participants with several different workshops within the Jamboree theme "Simply Scouting". About 40 000 Scouts and guides from 157 countries gathered at Rinkaby fields in Kristianstad in the south of Sweden, doubling the number of its inhabitants. The International Service Team staff (IST)

Richard Middelkoop

of the radio station counted 43 Scout radio operators from 13 different countries. About half came from Sweden and the other half from many different countries. The radio team worked in shifts to cover the full 24 hours per day on the radios.

Scandinavian sunset over SJ22S.

Swedish Radio Supply supported the station with ICOM transceivers and the local amateur radio club lend us portable antenna towers. The amateur radio station was built for 6 simultaneous operators and used an electronic log; quite sophisticated for the time. A computer at each transmitter logged the contacts onto a central server. From here, data were immediately uploaded to QRZ.com. Anyone could see from anywhere in the world on what frequencies we were active.

A great success was a portable HF station on a bicycle that toured all the sub camps to promote the Radio-Scouting programme. I also set up an information booth with another HF station at the WOSM section of the World Scout Centre.

The Jamboree also offered a rare personal moment. As it so happened, I had my entire family present there in different Scouting roles; my son as a participant, my oldest daughter and boyfriend working as IST at the camp, my XYL and youngest daughter as "special guest" visitors for the Bronze-Wolf luncheon and myself. It took a bit of organizing, but we managed a Scout family picture....

Many activities were on offer. At the entrance was a reception, with information panels of the Swedish amateur radio association, tables for Echolink, 2m and 70cm for local contacts and 80m. Next to it, the soldering work shop. We had 750 Dutch electronic kits available to build a battery tester. Furthermore we offered learning Morse code and how to send your own name and a foxhunt (on the 2 m band) over a challenging course through the woodlands. The main radio station offered Scouts a QSO, if possible with their home country.

The PA3BAR family at SJ22S.

The highlight was an activity using PMR handheld radios to guide a blindfolded Scout with a cup of water in his hand over an obstacle course. See how difficult it is to give directions via radio and not get wet.....

CQ Jamboree

Early 2014, I was already involved in getting the Scout operator team together for the *23rd World Scout Jamboree* in Japan. In February 2015, I was fortunate to attend a preparation meeting at the HQ of the Japanese Scout Association in Tokyo, where we coordinated the details of the programme. Some 33000 Scouts camped together on an immense camp site in Yamaguchi from 28 July to 8 August. Our amateur radio station was in place with the special call sign 8N23WSJ.

Swedish obstacle course guided by radio.

Due to a passing typhoon, the equipment could not be installed until just a few days before the start of the Jamboree. That was not the only WX challenge: each Jamboree day the temperature would go up to 45° C, occasionally even 52° C in the shade! Add a 90% humidity to that and you'll understand that cold camp showers were very popular.

The staff team consisted of an international group of Scout leaders from Japan, Zimbabwe, Philippines, Taiwan, Germany, Iceland, Finland, Australia, UK, Brazil, USA and The Netherlands.

400 Scouts visited the station each day and were offered a wide range of activities. Morse code practice, with a real Morse code paper tape writer, to take home as a souvenir. And a continued success from Sweden, the blind-folded obstacle course, where a participant had to carry water from one side to the other, whilst instructed by hand-held radio.

The fox hunting was done with regular FM transistor radios, which worked surprisingly well. The foxes were low-power transmitters with a range of about 10 meters, each producing a different sound. Introduction to digital radio modes like DSTAR and Echolink was on the menu, and of course, participation in the short-wave radio traffic.

All the equipment was provided for by ICOM,

8N23WSJ at the flatlands of Yamaguchi.

including an on-site service technician. During daytime it was not easy to get radio contacts out of Asia, but as soon as the sun started to set, the rest of the world was within reach.

One of the highlights was the scheduled direct contact between the International Space Station and the Jamboree. I managed to get the chairman of the World Scout Committee to be present as well as several WSB staff. We were able to see the ISS coming across the night sky, while we talked to the crew on board. 20 selected youth participants were all able to ask questions to the astronauts. This was a thrill. As one Colombian girl Scout asked me afterwards: "I just talked to an astronaut. How can I explain this to my mom and dad? They will never believe me....!"

Learning Morse code at 8N23WSJ.

In the main headquarter area of the camp, I set up a JOTA-JOTI promotion stand in the WOSM "better world" tent, together with my XYL. The stand attracted many international visitors, who could try their best in decoding Morse, listening to short-wave radio and playing with the electronic gadgets. Amongst the distinguished visitors were the Crown Prince of Japan and the Crown Prince of Saudi Arabia who tried out our electronics display as well. And packs of Japanese cub scouts enjoyed our famous tin-can telephone.

The *24th World Scout Jamboree* will be hosted by North-America (Canada, USA and Mexico) in 2019 in West-Virginia. For the Amateur Radio base the call sign NA1WJ has been secured. The goals are to introduce Scouts to science, technology, fun, and the magic of amateur radio operation. We'll also serve as the amateur-radio voice of the Jamboree via two-way radio contacts within the Jamboree and worldwide. NA1WJ will be an extensive demonstration station, offer ARDF Fox-hunting, and special events that include satellite contacts, an International Space Station contact, balloon launches, as well as low-power portable activation. Watch the radio bands for "North-America-1-World-Jamboree".

CQ Jamboree

A quick look into the future

Early 2018, the World JOTA-JOTI conducted an inspiring two-day session in Kuala Lumpur with an invited group of eight volunteers from National Scout Organisations around the globe, who joined with staff from the World Scout Bureau and the World Scout Committee to suggest future directions for the annual JOTA-JOTI activity; followed by an in-depth look at the event, its relevance for World Scouting and ways to raise it to the next level in the near future.

Building onto the strategy paper that I produced with the team the year before with the main themes "promote and encourage","changing the profile", and "innovative educational methods".

The workshop suggested avenues to support greater involvement of young people in the JOTA-JOTI weekend, to achieve a target of 3 million registered attendees involved by 2021 and make JOTA-JOTI available to as many young people as possible throughout the world.

A suggested action plan was developed. Specific areas proposed include a realignment of the JOTA-JOTI brand; enhance the educational framework of the activity including using theme driven, relevant educational activities each year linked to external specialist partners; having one centralised platform for JOTA-JOTI activities inside the scout.org ecosystem; encouraging group and individual registrations using a simplified process; building more effective 'safe from harm' mechanisms throughout the entire process; greater feedback processes; collecting data to validate the event; creating increased partnerships with external NGOs and corporate supporters; having ambassadors in regions and NSOs to promote and support implementation to achieve targets; and linking the event to other major global events where possible such as World Scout Jamborees.

The JOTA-JOTI event will be able to bring young Scouts together and engage in the larger discussion topics for future societies. After all, it will be their future. Imagine the impact in e.g. policy making on environmental aspects, international trade, dealing with conflicts and diversity inclusion if, no, when, a large forum of youngsters forms and expresses an opinion on these topic during JOTA-JOTI sessions; results that are then presented to UN decision makers e.g . They will take the "voice of the largest youth Movement on earth" into account; there's no way around it.

Societal trends play an important role. The past years, governments have put an emphasis on STEM education: Science, Technology, Engineering and Mathematics. And this trend will continue for another decade, no doubt. JOTA-JOTI provides an excellent opportunity to involve youngsters into a technical field of work; something that will absolutely be necessary to sustain the hunger of the future generations towards increased communication traffic and possibilities, in particular, the wireless ones. Radio amateurs could very well play a vital role in this informal education. Their enthusiasm, unconventional solutions and technical know-how seem compatible with the Scout programme in this respect. JOTA-JOTI offers an excellent learning experience for Scouts, a technical training in an informal, playful way, which is fun to do.

The existing mobile communication means make almost everyone reachable anywhere at any time. It facilitates having a conversation or exchange with a Scout somewhere else, be it at the other end of town, or in another country. We take that for granted, until…...right, until something happens and part of the infrastructure is lost. Then it all of a sudden becomes apparent how dependent everybody has become on the global presence of communications means; you don't miss it, until it's gone.

JOTA-JOTI offers element to focus on the "emergency preparedness" aspect, the tricks Scouts can do if anything else fails. An important asset will be the creativity and ingenuity of young Scouts that think "out of the box" and come up with all sorts of new applications and solutions. What presents itself as a problem, is rather a challenge to them.

Bringing together many Scouts from different cultures is not even special anymore; the multi-cultural societies made this something of everyday live. The element of belonging together as one Movement will always remain and in this respect the JOTA-JOTI event will continue to play a major role. Even more so through growing the participation to double or triple today's numbers and making the event available to as many Scouts as we possibly can.

JOTA: what started as a small idea in the cafeteria at the Sutton Coldfield World Scout Jamboree in 1957, has grown into the largest WOSM event on the annual calendar. During its existence, JOTA brought together millions of Scouts, created new and lasting friendships, built new networks, provided technical resources and emergency help during disasters and contributed to a better understanding of each other's culture and way of live. It could continue to do so in the years to come, for future generations to enjoy and benefit. Many Scouts could be part of it. Will you?

This historic overview is dedicated to the National JOTA-JOTI Coordinators, volunteer Scout leaders, National radio-licensing Authorities, World Scout Bureau staff members, IRC network volunteers, service providers and the ten-thousands of radio amateurs who make JOTA-JOTI possible each year for the benefit of young Scouts to explore the World.

Richard Middelkoop, PA3BAR
World JOTA-JOTI Organizer
May 2018.

CQ Jamboree

Amateur Radio and Scouting Language

as you will find it throughout this book

band	set of radio wavelengths allocated to radio amateurs
Brownsea	island in the UK where the first Scout camp was held by Baden Powell in August 1907
call sign	identification number of an amateur radio station
conditions	the ability of the ionosphere to guide radio waves around the world
contest	competition to make the most radio contacts
CQ	general call to find another radio station and make contact
CW	radio transmission in Morse code
DX	long distance radio contact
Echolink	a system that relays amateur radio signals over the internet
Fox hunt	finding a hidden radio transmitter using a directional receiver to take bearings.
GMT	Greenwich Mean Time
Jamboree	large international gathering of Scouts
JOTA-JOTI	Jamboree On The Air – Jamboree On The Internet
log	list of contacted stations, with some technical details
Net	get-together of more radio stations on the same wavelength
NJC	National JOTA-JOTI Coordinator
QRM	interference during a radio transmission
QRT	end of transmissions
QSL card	a postcard with technical data sent to confirm a radio contact
QSO	a contact between two or more radio stations
QTH	place from where a radio station is transmitting
RTTY	radio transmission using telex
SK	Silent Key, radio amateur who passed away
sked	pre-arranged time to meet on the air
SSTV	slow-scan television pictures for world-wide transmission

wireless	a connection between two radio stations, (however, usually requiring a lot of wires locally)
WJJT	World JOTA-JOTI Team, a team of volunteers organizing the JOTA-JOTI event annually
WOSM	World Organization of the Scout Movement
WSB	World Scout Bureau, the headquarters of WOSM (formerly in London, later in Ottawa, next in Geneva, now in Kuala Lumpur)
XYL	ex young lady: wife of a radio amateur

www.ingramcontent.com/pod-product-compliance
Lightning Source LLC
Chambersburg PA
CBHW041622220426
43662CB00001B/24